He Opens He's Eyes
and
He Closes He's Eyes

by

Terri Powers

Bloomington, IN   Milton Keynes, UK

authorHOUSE®

AuthorHouse™
1663 Liberty Drive, Suite 200
Bloomington, IN 47403
www.authorhouse.com
Phone: 1-800-839-8640

AuthorHouse™ UK Ltd.
500 Avebury Boulevard
Central Milton Keynes, MK9 2BE
www.authorhouse.co.uk
Phone: 08001974150

First published by AuthorHouse 2/12/2007

ISBN: 978-1-4259-8867-8 (sc)

Library of Congress Control Number: 2006911202

Printed in the United States of America
Bloomington, Indiana

This book is printed on acid-free paper.

Contents

1. Kiddie Perceptions – Misunderstandings & Genius .. 1
2. The Consequences of Being a Silent Observer 6
3. Early Automation in the Department Store 18
4. Speaking of Tongues 19
5. Homework Wars 20
6. So Long, Maid Lady! 22
7. It Rolled off My Tongue 26
8. Color My Head Phitty 28
9. Fanny in the Daytime – Monster at Night 31
10. Basement Games 34
11. Poison Ivy, Grass Stains, Mushrooms, and
    Other Strange Things 41
12. What Comes After Wednesday? 44
13. The Unsolved Mysteries of the Boxer and
    the Horse 47
14. Back in the Dogwood House Again 52
15. The Crabby Apple Dog 54
16. Washing My Own Mouth with Soap 58
17. River of Syrup, Pool of BBQ Sauce 60
18. Grandpa's House 64
19. Grandma's Toy Drawer 68
20. Grandma Meets Woody Woodpecker 72
21. They Lay Out Dead Horses, Don't They? 74
22. Who Started this Punny Business? 77
23. My Name's Red – I Live Near the Meat District 80
24. We Don't Smile in my Profession 82
25. Do Teeth Give Your Brown Bat Gas? 84

26. I Hate Socks 88

27. Pinecone Energy 93

28. The Story Behind "Dickie's in the Back
    Seat Barfin'" 96

29. I'm on a Different Plane 100

30. Monster Hands 105

31. The Quest For the Perfect Concrete Turtle 108

32. Learning to Ride a Bike 110

33. How Much Faith Does it Take to Pierce a Rock? .. 116

34. Eyeing the Girls 119

35. I've Gone to Pot at Age 8 121

36. No, Really - What's For Dessert? 126

37. Knowing Who Your Marbles Are 129

38. Must Be that Dairy Air! 135

39. I'm Pool Guy, the Everything Man!
    (Toot! Toot!) 137

40. Invention of the Worm Maker 143

41. Somebody's Gonna Need an Ambulance! 146

42. Age Requirement at the Post Office 148

43. Spurting my Juices 150

44. You Can Always Depend on Frank 152

45. Going Courting 154

46. Fighting Fire with Fire Before the Fire 156

47. Seeing Stars at the Movies 161

48. Waxing Poetic 164

49. Always Acknowledge Cat Trophies
    Immediately! 166

50. Picture This! 169

51. Don't Put Flatware in the Washing Machine 174

52. Pizza Junk 179

53. Bookworms and Crawly Things Always
    Catch Up 184
54. Purple Cow Products 188

1. Kiddie Perceptions –
Misunderstandings & Genius

There is a certain way that many kids interpret various situations, and often they keep these thoughts a secret for years as they try to figure them out silently on their own. Much confusion on their part would be saved if they would just ask an adult about the event at hand, but many times, the adults never hear about it until years after the kid has figured out what was really going on. I remember a lot of these happenings from my childhood, and heard about a number of them from my siblings' early days as well. I call these observations and self-speculations "Kiddie Perceptions". I have detailed a number of these in separate essays for this book.

There are other types of Kiddie Perceptions as well, such as the way babies manage to figure things out on their own that you might think of as confusing. Take dogs, for instance. With over 200 recognized breeds, how does a young child know when he's seeing a "doggie"? Yes, he may have been coached by a parent the first few times, but do all breeds look alike? Does a Maltese look like a German Shepherd? Does a Malamute look like a Chihuahua? No, I'd say the pictures of Malamutes I've seen look more like bears. And what about Bedlington Terriers? They look like lambs. And who would think that an Old English Sheep Dog looks like a Mexican Hairless? Yet, a child just learning to talk will spot a "doggie" out a car window before you do, every time, no matter what the breed.

Speaking of dogs, and while we're at it, cats, there was another thing that always puzzled me when I was about 4 or 5. Why did female animals have whiskers? In other words, if the dog up the street was a girl, as I'd been told, why did she have a mustache? And if the cat next door was female, what was she doing sporting handlebars? I never could understand that. Of course, at that time, I had not yet met my fourth grade teacher, a nun with a prominent black mustache. That might have made these ideas a little easier to grasp. Except, there was still the fact that all of the female animals I knew had whiskers, and only a few of the female humans did.

And speaking of whiskers, did you ever notice that the pulp in lemonade looks like something you might find in the bathroom sink after a good beard trim? I always had a hard time drinking the stuff because of the hair floating in the top.

And why did people take Bear aspirin? I saw and heard enough commercials for them, so they must exist. If they were for bears, why were they showing them on TV as if they were for human use? Did bears watch TV? And do bears get headaches, or, as the commercials suggest now, heart attacks? How do you tell when a bear has a headache, anyway? They can be nasty enough without one. And how do you give a bear an aspirin without losing an arm - put the sucker in a fish and throw it?

Another thing I often found myself doing was refusing to believe my ears when someone told me I could help myself to something. I was sure I had heard wrong, and as soon as I reached for the offered item, I would have my hand slapped, and hear, "I didn't say you could have that!" I didn't want to risk the embarrassment of getting my hopes up and then being reprimanded. Since I didn't talk to many adults when I was a kid, I couldn't explain this, and they were often puzzled. I can think of 3 examples.

Behind the house next door to us lived three elderly ladies, widowed sisters who had all moved in together after being left alone. This was back in the days when you didn't have to watch out for homemade treats on Halloween. You could accept anything without fear of being poisoned, drugged or maimed. These ladies sometimes made popcorn balls, which I'm sure, must have taken a lot of work.

One year I was a witch (watch it, now!) and had a costume made by my mom from a pattern. That's when I first discovered that black fabric sometimes smells horrible and the dye smell takes a while to dissipate. It was a large cape that went over a black skirt and blouse, or maybe a one-piece dress.

When we got back to the next street and approached the old ladies' house, they held out the large plate with wrapped popcorn balls, allowing each of the kids to take their own. But I couldn't. I was sure it was a trick. After a lot of urging, one of the ladies finally suggested to her sister that maybe I couldn't reach out from under the oversized cape. She picked one out for me, dropped it in my bag, and I went on. Ah, kind and gentle lady; I was saved by the belle.

Another time I was at a neighbor's house with my mom, and the family had purchased some tiny ice cream cones. I had never seen that size, before or since. It was a hot day, and they had gone out to the picnic table on the screened-in porch or sunroom in back of the house. The ice cream and the cones were taken out there, and they were each making their own. That was a big family – about 11 or 12 kids, and they had at least one more after we moved. Their mother suggested that one of her older girls make up a cone for me. It was set before me on the picnic table, but I couldn't make myself reach for it. I was dying for it, but didn't know if it was really mine or not. Finally, after it melted and ran down the side of the cone, making a thick gooey river on the table, someone decided to take it away. It looked like I didn't want it, and it could only get worse on the table. I missed out on that one.

I also may have missed out on the third example I'm thinking about. This was in fourth grade. My teacher had bought or been given a very large box of chocolates, which she decided to pass around the room. It may have been just before Christmas. She told us to each take one piece and pass the box to the person in front of us. The box eventually came to me, but I couldn't take one. Other kids were getting impatient that I wasn't passing it on; just letting it sit on the corner of my desk. My teacher, an old-fashioned nun, yelled at me that I should just send it on if I didn't want any. She must have thought I was trying to hoard the whole box, or she just didn't want to deal with finding out why I was doing this. I wasn't trying to cause trouble; I was truly afraid in each of these instances that I was somehow being tested, and would catch it big-time if I failed and succumbed to taking something that wasn't mine. I don't remember if I didn't get any candy that time, or if someone just set a piece on my desk and continued the box on its trek around the room.

Another example of a Kiddie Perception I experienced had to do with taking the script of a TV show seriously. Some may remember the old cartoon, called Yakky Doodle. Yakky was a duck, and his best friend was a tough-looking, but gentle bulldog who often gave him advice and comfort. In this particular episode, which I saw when I was about 4 Yakky Doodle was upset because he wanted to be on television, and couldn't figure out how to break into the business. His dog friend consoled him, and I think he finally did get to be on television. But, at that young age, the question kept bugging me, "Why doesn't he know he's already on television? I'm watching him! What's he talking about?" Only when I saw that same episode about 10 years later did I realize it was just part of the story line in that day's cartoon.

A warning to kids who may not have learned…*Never* repeat a word you've heard casually in the neighborhood, at school or wherever. Find out what it means first. You could save some teeth, or at least avoid some anger.

I remember one night when I was about 7 or 8 we had some potatoes at dinner that I thought were extremely terrible. I don't know how they'd been prepared (besides boiling them) or what was on them, but they tasted nasty. I had heard a word somewhere, I don't remember where, and I figured from its use that it was just another fancy way of saying "crummy". I thought maybe I could impress my family with my new vocabulary, and also voice my dissatisfaction with the choice of side-dish for that evening. I sat next to my dad at the table at that time. A bad choice of seating arrangements, it turned out, considering what was to come. Launching myself on my linguistics debut, I announced, "These potatoes are crappy!" and promptly received a set of hairy knuckles in my mouth. You want fries with that? Well, yeah, they would be better than these potatoes. I quickly figured out that there must be another meaning to that word, but it was awhile before I found it out.

Another thing that doesn't really qualify as a Kiddie Perception, but does indirectly, is when something is done by an adult in such a ridiculous manner that it might as well have been laid out by a kid. I have a couple of these in this book, and, I grimace to say, I was the one who did these things later in life. And I paid the price for doing them.

And one more type of Kiddie Perception has to do with adults who purposely act silly as if they don't know any better. This is commonly known as a "second childhood" and is also covered in this book. My grandma was a good example of that, in one instance. Hopefully you will see yourself, or someone you know in these stories, and it will help you to understand more about the world through the eyes of a child and beyond. Just so you don't start doing these things as a regular practice!

2. The Consequences of Being a Silent Observer

"Mommy! She has a coat just like mine!" a neighbor girl exclaimed when she saw me.

The kitchen erupted with the laughter of the ladies who were having coffee together that morning.

"I was wondering," the girl's mother answered. "Julie Nabors has a coat like yours too!"

The laughter started up again, and the girl who had made the exuberant statement looked confused.

In our neighborhood, the passing down of outgrown clothes from one family to another was traditional. Often, a garment would make the rounds of the neighborhood, eventually to return to the original household to be used by a younger sibling who was now ready for it.

The coat I was wearing that morning was red with accents of black and white trim down the front. Evidently, I was at least the third owner of this coat.

I had observed a lot of these kinds of interactions between parents and their kids, and it seemed that more often than not, the parents ended up laughing at whatever their kids had said. It was all in innocence to be sure; they were not exactly laughing "at" the kids. That's just the way a lot of adults react to the ways of childish language.

What bothered me though, was the fact that these parents never noticed the looks on their kids' faces when this would happen. Often these kids would be standing there looking confused and/or upset and I would just be sitting there wondering what these ladies were laughing about.

The direct confrontations like this one were the worst, but often this same type of event would happen subtly. A story about a neighbor kid could float around the neighborhood for weeks with a different group of people laughing each time it was told.

I remember a kid named Margie who was one of my best friends before and during my kindergarten year. Various people had observed that Margie had suddenly begun walking strangely. She would walk stiffly, rocking back and forth on her feet as if on stilts. Her parents became concerned that there was something wrong with her feet or legs. When questioned about it, her reply was simply, "I don't want to get those creases in my new shoes!"

My young mind perceived this as a very normal thing, and again, I couldn't see what the fuss was all about.

I remember also, the lady who gleefully told everyone in the neighborhood who would listen, what her son was giving his father for Father's Day. "I'm gonna be good for another week – just like I gave you last time!"

I could just see that kid, cringing and counting the days until he could stop being good, after having that story spread all over.

I know there were times when I could have said something that would have set these people off. But I usually made sure I kept it in so I wouldn't have to deal with them laughing at me. One example of this was the way I interpreted the song, "Yankee Doodle". I liked the part about "with the girls be candy." It sounded good to me that the girls would get all the candy, and the boys, none. But I never brought it up.

Rather, my reaction to all of this was to clam up whenever there were any adults around. I talked at home, but even that was controlled, because the teasing attitude was prevalent there also.

Often if I wanted something, I would ask for it in pantomime, especially if the neighbors or any other adults were present. Even if there was somebody in the room that I normally did talk to, I wasn't going to let those other people hear me. That way they couldn't go off and repeat any stories about *me!*

The result of this was that I was sent to doctors. From the time I was three, off and on until I was nineteen, I was bounced around from one doctor to the next. The doctors labeled me retarded, autistic, schizophrenic, etc. Considering some of the characters I was stuck in front of, I think a lot of times the glue was on the wrong side of the label!

My parents knew these labels didn't fit me. This is one of the reasons I got so many different doctors. As soon as I would get a label from one doctor, I would get another doctor.

As if all of these psychiatrists and psychologists weren't enough for me, there were a few reasons for me to be seeing other types of doctors. From the time I was in fourth grade until about 18 years ago, I was getting anywhere from one to four ear infections every year. Also, from the time I was three until I was twelve, I was constantly getting bladder infections. It wasn't long before I was running away from anyone wearing a white coat.

The first doctor I went to for the bladder infections used to torture me by dilating me every time I went to see him. I would scream and have to be held down, and it seemed to go on forever. He must have known that he was doing something that was highly uncomfortable to his patients because each time before I left his office he would write me a prescription for an ice cream cone. He had a deal worked out with a certain drug store; he'd write a prescription which I would take into this store, and they would give me a free ice cream cone! There was also a drug prescription involved, but they'd fill the ice cream one first so I'd have something to do while I was waiting. I never did know if the doctor settled the account with them every month or so, or if this was just that drug store's way of getting business, and the doctors didn't have to pay for it.

I remember leaving this doctor's office once in the middle of winter (in Kansas!) and going for my ice cream cone. A lady who was a customer in the drug store looked at me and said, "Too cold for an ice cream cone!" What did she know? Her kid was eating a candy bar, and she probably had to pay for it. I wasn't going to let all the snow in Kansas stop me from eating free chocolate in any form!

The only doctor from my early days that I can remember treating me right was a urologist I had right after we moved to California. This guy lived right behind us. One time when they were barbecuing hamburgers in their yard, he asked my parents to boost me over the fence so he could give me one. Another time he came to our house with his wife for an evening with my parents. He saw me in another room and kept coaxing me to come out and visit with them. He didn't know that I had been told to stay away and leave them alone while they were visiting. He couldn't figure out why I wouldn't come in.

This doctor knew the importance of not upsetting his patients. So many doctors will either discuss things in front of kids or send them out of the room to wait alone and worry while they talk to the parents. Most people think these are the only choices. But this doctor knew what to do.

An elderly lady named Bertha, everybody's perfect grandma, was this doctor's nurse. Whenever the doctor wanted to talk to my mother alone, Bertha would keep me occupied in the other room. Somehow this attention made up for the fact that I knew they were talking about me in the doctor's office. Bertha knew her distracting methods well, and on the day I found out she was leaving this doctor, I felt that I really was losing a grandma.

This doctor's oldest son was in my fifth grade class. I didn't realize he noticed anything I did. One day I learned in his father's office that he had come home from school and reported that I was one of the smartest kids in the class. Huh! I had always thought that about him!

The only people in Kansas who really knew what was going on with me were the kids of the neighborhood and my kindergarten class. They used to tell everyone, "Theresa's shy." Of course, the adults scoffed this away. They "knew" there was more to it than that. But those kids were right. That's all it ever was. There was a reason none of my doctors was able to find anything wrong – there was nothing to find! Maybe they didn't teach that where these doctors went to school.

One thing that came out of all these medical observations was that I started to feel like I was under a microscope. What could I do but stiffen up and talk less? I believe I would have come out of all of this a lot sooner if I'd been left alone to work it out. But nobody knew what was going on.

Different people tried different methods to get me to talk. A man who lived next door to us always used to say to me, "I heard you talking last night." I didn't believe him; he may have been trying to catch me off guard so I would answer him; he may have thought I'd give up and start talking since he had supposedly "heard" me anyway. In any case, I never fell for it.

There was one lady who could always figure out what I was trying to say with my pantomiming. But she tried to hide it because she wanted me to talk. She didn't want to encourage me to keep up the mime act. She used to say to me all the time, "You'll have to talk to *me*, because... *I* can't *hear* you!" Same inflection every time. And I'd think, "Well, then ... what good's it gonna do if I talk?"

You know, she even taught her kids to say that one? It blew my mind the day I heard her nine-year-old daughter say to me in the same tone, "You'll have to talk to *me*, because... *I* can't *hear* you!" I couldn't believe it.

I know, also, that there have been times that I've been guilty of inadvertently doing the same things to kids as I've gotten older. Usually, in more recent years, if I've found myself starting to laugh at something a kid is doing or saying, I've tried to hide and stifle the response, sometimes by looking into the other room and covering my mouth a bit. I did have one experience, though, when I may have let go of it in front of a couple of kids. I don't remember exactly how I handled it, or if it was noticed by them.

It was when I was about sixteen or seventeen. I was in a now defunct, somewhat upscale department store with my mom. I don't remember what we originally went there for, but when we were finished with our intended errand, my mom asked me if I wanted to look at anything else, like maybe the toy department. This was in the days when department stores still *had* toy departments and also in the days when people could still leave their kids in one department and shop in the other without fear of harm or crime befalling their kids. People don't dare do that now.

I have always been crazy about toys, and have often had kids gravitate to me because I'm the only adult they know who will stop and play with them when I'm visiting one of their parents. Most kids learn early on that "mom's friends aren't interested in what I'm playing with" and it blows them away when they find out someone will look at their toys. Therefore, it wasn't surprising at all that my mom would suggest the toy department when I was in my late teens.

On this day, we headed to the upstairs of this department store to look at what toys they had. In one aisle, a small boy and a slightly older girl, maybe three and four or four and five years old were playing together with no adults in sight. The boy had taken down a kiddie car and was sitting on it. The girl decided to razz him about playing with a toy he was too old for. In the classic nyeah-nyeah singsong melody,

11

she danced slightly, pointed at him and sang, "Look! He's a baby!"

The boy quickly got off the toy vehicle and stood tall and indignant, facing the girl. In a situation torn between defending his manhood and breaking into tears, he informed her, "**Oy** yam *notta bay*-bee!"

My mom and I could barely contain ourselves, and may have laughed right on the spot, or maybe we ducked into another aisle to hide it. I don't remember if the kids noticed us, but I know now that this was a similar situation to what I saw happening over and over when I was a kid.

Also, there was one time when I allowed others to laugh at something I'd said, mainly because I thought it was funny too. Arriving in St. Louis one day on one of our many trips there, I noticed a sign on the front of one of the stores in the crowded area we were driving through. The sign had probably been there for years, but this time I knew how to read. The sign said, "Budweiser", which I had heard of many times, especially since my uncle worked for Anheuser-Busch from the time he was a teenager until his retirement. But this was the first time I realized that the name wasn't "Bugweiser". I had wondered what they put in their beer. My mom decided we definitely needed to tell her brother what I had always thought his product was made of. The announcement was made in front of a bunch of my relatives who we happened to be visiting with one day; I believe it was my grandma and grandpa's house, where my aunt and uncle had come to visit with us. Everybody thought it was hilarious. Just think, years later they could have had a commercial in which someone would say, "Thanks, but I wanted a Bug Light!" Then they could have gotten zapped.

Within the year before I started kindergarten, there was a program in the local newspaper on teaching your kids how to read at home. My mother taught me how to read when I was about 4 years old, before I started school. She had a couple of reasons for doing this. Not only was it good for me to learn how to read, but she had talked to the parents of some of the kids who were going to be in my class, and she knew that they weren't teaching their kids with this program. Her idea was that if I started school and was the only one in the class who knew how to read, they wouldn't be able to shut me up. I would be popping up with all the answers and be cured. Good idea, huh? It was certainly worth a try. But it didn't come out that way. As it turned out, I went through my entire year of kindergarten without saying a single word to my teacher. That blew everybody's minds. More doctors!

In later years, when I was about six, there were two couples in the neighborhood who I did talk to. These were people who had proven to me that they weren't going to be like all the others. I could see that they listened to kids, they talked to them, and they didn't treat them like "dumb little kids".

This is not to say that they treated the kids like adults. I have seen far too much of that in recent years. T.V. shows seem to have been encouraging this practice for years. It doesn't work any more than talking down to them. But these two couples in my neighborhood knew exactly how to get on the kids' level and talk directly to them. This is all too rare.

One of these couples lived right across the street from us. They were young and had no children yet, but they were crazy about kids. Everybody liked to go over to Greg & Kathy's house. I used to spend hours over there, and often came home carrying something they wanted to give away. They did a lot of traveling, and their house was full of all sorts of trinkets and souvenirs. I had straw ladies and donkeys from Mexico, a wooden rooster, a ceramic turtle, three ceramic cats with fur glued to the legs and heads and a whole collection of plastic swizzle sticks from all over!

These people had a cat named Lisa who had kittens. They kept one of the kittens and named him Charger. The story behind this was that they knew someone who worked for Dodge, and the guy couldn't stand cats. They thought it would be funny to name their cat after a Dodge car model.

I stayed away from the cats in their house unless someone else was around. There was a reason for this. As is the basic theme of this book, a lot of adults will say things to kids without realizing how the child's mind perceives them. Since I didn't talk around most people, I often heard the question, "cat got your tongue?" I really thought that cats had the power to rip peoples' tongues out. And I wondered if they had a taste for tongues; maybe that's what cat food was made from.

Once when I was at Greg & Kathy's house, their cat, Charger was on the table in the dining room. Kathy had gone to take out the trash or something, and I was alone in the room with the cat. For some reason, on impulse, I stuck out my tongue at Charger. Within a split second of doing so, I remembered those words, "Cat got your tongue?" I was filled with fear. It seemed that this cat had begun staring at me as soon as I had done that. Now that he knew I had a tongue, I was sure that he would shoot across the room and yank it out of me. I ran out of the room and went to find Kathy.

The other couple I talked to lived up the street and had seven kids. They better know how to talk to kids! Again, they would ask me questions and talk directly to me instead of talking down to me.

Once when I was riding my skateboard down the sidewalk, (sitting down), they stopped to talk to me. I showed them a sticker that I had put on my skateboard, and they read it out loud. It said, "Please Fasten Seat Belt." They thought it was funny. My dad worked for the phone company, and their picnics every year were called "Safety Fairs". That's where I got the sticker.

Even though people laughed at my sticker, it didn't bother me the way it did when the other neighbors laughed at kids. The sticker on the skateboard was meant to be funny. What bothered me was when the adults would take a kid's innocent comments and turn them into a neighborhood joke, never seeming to notice how it affected their kids.

Looking back, I can think of a few other people in the neighborhood who I would like to have talked to. I'm not sure why I didn't. Maybe I had just gotten to a point of not being able to trust too many people at one time.

The lady who could always figure out my pantomiming is one example of someone I'd like to meet up with again. Back in the '80s I made a serious effort to get her address from the phone books at the library. This was long before the internet. But she'd moved often and I couldn't track her down. I had wanted to write her and explain the reasons for what I had done, and also to let her know that I'd always thought she was nice. I could just picture myself standing around gabbing with her in her kitchen just like I did with Greg and Kathy. I wonder why I always put her on the side with "those other people"! Maybe it was for the simple reason that she was making an effort to "make me talk". I do know that whenever I sensed this sort of thing taking place, no matter who was doing it, I immediately felt put in the spotlight, and that made it even harder to start talking to people.

Four houses down from us lived an elderly couple named Bob and Annette. These were some more people I should have spent more time around. They would have been good ones to talk to. There is no way to contact them now, as they have both been deceased for years.

I remember that they seemed to do a lot of yard work. I used to see Bob raking leaves, and Annette pulling weeds.

Often when I would walk by their house, Bob would stop what he was doing, straighten up, and look at me. He would always say, "Well, well, well!" as he shook his head slowly, and a grin spread across his face.

Once when I was at their house with my mother, he gave me three marshmallow peanuts and some of those tiny Hershey bars. I'm not sure if he told me to share them with my brothers and sister, or if my mother made me do it. But I remember Bob saying something about my eyes shining when he handed them to me. They would have made great grandparents, but for some reason they never had any kids. I never knew why. One time when I was in their house, I whispered in my mother's ear, "Where are the kids?" She told me they didn't have any, and Annette smiled at me. It seemed so unusual to me that someone wouldn't have any kids, especially since there were families all around the neighborhood who had seven or eight. One family had ten or eleven! Too bad their mother was one of the ones who laughed the loudest at what her kids said. Hopefully, she knows better now. She probably has some grandchildren.

It is continually amazing to me the things that people will say in front of you when they think you don't know what's going on. They'll speak freely! You can learn a lot when people think you're nuts, because they'll say anything with you in the room. They figure it's not going to stick. *Now* who's retarded?

I can think of a teacher who made an announcement to the entire class that I was brain-damaged. **Rrrrrt!!!** **WRONG!!!** Good thing she wasn't my everyday teacher.

I remember a nurse who asked me a question one day when I was in having some extensive tests for the many bladder infections I used to get. I didn't answer her. She looked at another nurse in the room, and the second one tapped her head saying, "Oh, she's…," indicating that I was mentally unsound. **Zzzztt!! WRONG ANSWER!!** Sit down!!

And then there was one of my sixth grade teachers, the one who was a little weird anyway. She used to tell us creepy stories; where she got them, I never knew. She was like the tabloid reporter of that school, telling us the grossest stuff she could dig up. Some were claimed to be personal experiences of kids she had taught; others sounded like trash newspaper articles. She also taught classes in seventh and eighth grade, and spread her stories throughout all of these classes.

We heard about the kid in one of her classes who leaned on a metal-edged ruler with his teeth, and it slipped and cut his nose in half. And the one who got half of a baseball bat stuck in his forehead on the playground, resulting in a metal plate being placed in his head. She didn't say if it was Home Plate. She told the eighth grade, my brother's class, about a lady who cut up her husband and cooked him. We didn't hear whether she ate him. So we never found out if he was a good husband, a tough man or a person of good taste. I wasn't in that class, so I never heard that whole story; just a short recitation from a student in my carpool.

There were times when she would be chewing out the class over something they had done wrong. She would scream and rant, detailing all the things they needed to change. And in the middle of all this, she would point out, "even Theresa Powers knows better!" As if this was to convey that any moron could figure this out.

And even Theresa Powers knew that this was that teacher's last year there, too! I think the principal got a lot of complaints about her; some were most likely from parents, who'd had to assure their kids that the Zodiac Killer probably *wouldn't* get them on Halloween, no matter what their mentor of education had warned.

One of the many teachers we were better off without.

3. Early Automation in the Department Store

So much is hidden in the minds of kids, not to be revealed until years later, if ever. This has been evidenced many times for me, not only in my own experience, but with others who have suddenly brought up incidents from their own younger years. Who would have known, for example, that my oldest brother was afraid to go into the Sears department store as a kid, if he hadn't mentioned it 30 or 40 years later?

My brother was especially wary of a certain partially walled-in area next to the escalators. There may have been plants in there for decoration, but what else might be lurking in there? Well, in my brother's mind, it was a scary metallic automated creature known as the Sears Robot.

Commercials and other references to this store often made mention of Sears, Roebuck & Co. My brother heard differently. And he was always on the lookout for this monster, which could easily resemble some of the stuff he'd seen in movies or read about. He wasn't about to be picked up and carried off by this piece of machinery.

He never mentioned this until he was at least in his 40s. It seemed that this area by the escalators was the most likely place in his mind for this thing to be hanging out, waiting to grab some unsuspecting kid. He always stuck close to whatever adult he had accompanied on this trip, making sure to remain alive and whole. If only he had brought up the subject earlier, or at least seen an ad that would have had the name spelled out, he may have been saved some fear in those early years.

I don't know when he found out the truth. Maybe learning to read had something to do with it. However it may have happened, the Sears robot was disassembled and put away for a long time.

4. Speaking of Tongues

Was it a case of bad hearing or bad enunciation? Most likely, it was an example of a kid hearing an expression for the first time. Either that or my middle brother was a genius at a very early age, and good at hiding mischievous behavior. I believe it was the former, a new group of words hitting his young ears for the first time.

My brother was about 2, or maybe 3. He was sitting on my mom's lap, telling her some kind of wild story he made up on the spur of the moment. It got more unbelievable by the second. At least he showed some creativity in his early years. But my mom knew he was bluffing, or at least teasing her. She bit the bait, and returned in kind.

"Look me in the eye when you say that!" she faced him playfully, in mock sternness.

My brother was confused at this collection of words. "Huh?" he said, stopping his story and wrinkling his forehead at her.

My mom repeated, "Look me in the eye!"

Well, if she really wanted it! My brother quickly complied by leaning toward her, sticking out his tongue, and licking her right smack in the eye!

My mom was surprised beyond belief. "What'd you do that for?"

My brother, in complete childlike innocence, answered her, "You told me to!"

Ask, and ye shall receive! And next time, enunciate, or at least explain yourself beforehand!

5. Homework Wars

Same brother, different year... This guy sure did have a penchant for getting into things, whether innocently or on purpose. Trouble was, we were never sure which time was which.

This was the same brother who had taken a trip down the storm drain, as mentioned in my last book. Other events included absent-mindedly taking my mom's car keys to school, playing hooky from kindergarten and pumping hard on the pedals of a two-wheeler with no brakes as he zoomed down a hill on our street. Before this last mentioned event took place, he had come into the house asking my mom to come out and "see what I can do". She was several months pregnant at the time, but she came out to watch. As soon as she saw what he was doing, she freaked out and went dashing down the sidewalk after him. Just as she was about to catch up with him, my brother rode up onto the sidewalk, coasted onto somebody's lawn and turned the bike on its side, standing up with his arms held triumphantly in the air. Ta-da! My mom stood on that lawn, panting for awhile. It's a wonder she didn't deliver prematurely. My brother didn't know for many years after, that this bike never had any brakes. He had practiced this feat, and knew what he was doing before he called her out there.

Homework was always a major battle with him; there were often things he didn't understand, (such as spelling words), and somehow, when my mom would be helping him, her explanations didn't always get through his head. His teacher wanted the students to write sentences with the spelling words; rather than just showing they could spell them, she wanted proof that they knew how to use them.

My mom would have him use the dictionary, or at least she would come up with a definition or two to explain it to him. Still, there were a lot of erasures, as he would write sentences that didn't quite make the true meaning of the word, proving he didn't understand.

Most often, he would turn in papers with dirty eraser marks and numerous tearstains. My mother often wondered if the teacher thought he was being abused at home.

Then one day, he had the word, "shrew". This was a new one! What did that mean? A quick check with the dictionary revealed the definition, something to the tune of, "a miserable, nagging woman".

Aha! My brother, finally understanding, buckled down to his work and wrote on his paper, "My mother is a shrew."

She let him go with it. She'd fought him long enough.

6. So Long, Maid Lady!

When I was a tyke, around 3 to 6 years old, I would often play with my toys in the middle of the living room floor. I did have a room I shared with my sister upstairs, and we also had a basement that had been turned into sort of a playroom. But it was fun to sometimes scatter things in the middle of the living room floor and just mess around. Especially when the rest of the family was there, maybe in the evening, reading the paper, books, or just messing around themselves.

And when I would be done playing, or just get bored, I would look at my toys arranged haphazardly in the middle of the floor. For a brief moment, I would consider picking them up, as I knew I should. Then, silently, in my head, I would say, "They can do it!" and leave the room.

I didn't tell anyone about this for years. Instead, unknown to me, my parents were allowed to believe I was just a lazy slob who left everything to them. It was many years, probably when I was in my mid-20's that I finally mentioned it.

When I did tell, their reaction was, "what a brat!"

But I wasn't a brat! I really wasn't! I'm not! Am not! Am not!

What was really happening was this: in our neighborhood and especially within our church, people had a way of looking after each other, mainly in times of dire need, but generally, at all times. There was a program, run through our church that was called "Circles". They were small groups of volunteers from the church that were formed for the purpose of taking care of their own neighborhoods. Everybody in one circle was from one neighborhood. Their own area was their responsibility. The circles were numbered to distinguish one group from the other. Our neighborhood had Circle 15.

Whenever anyone had a major event or tragedy in the family, a circle meeting would be called in their area. People would sign up to bring food for the evening meal for as long as the family needed it. It was very organized; a different person would sign up for a different part of the meal every night, and would say what they were bringing. That kept a family from getting 14 potato salads and 28 desserts. Although, I might have liked that!

This was done for such happenings as a death in a family, a family member in the hospital or any other big deal. I remember once, a girl that my sister knew from school had her house burn down. I don't think she lived in our area, but I do remember being driven past the house to look at it. I'm sure that family got help from whatever circle covered their area.

I don't know how much my own family got involved in the circles before 1960. But I do know that they got into it heavily after that. Because there was a time in early 1960 when we had 2 family members in 2 separate hospitals, in 2 separate cities in 2 separate states at the same time. I was in a Missouri hospital with spinal meningitis, and my mom was in a Kansas hospital with lymph edema. Circle 15 stepped in, in a big way for my family for quite a while during that time.

There really was a lot of food involved in this. Sometimes the recipients would be so overwhelmed that they would have to call up the chairman and say, "why don't you hold off a few days while we eat leftovers?" Then, when they needed more, it would start up again.

Often, people would say things like, "how are we going to repay all of those people? That's a lot of people who did something for us – how do you get back to each one?" Well, you don't need to. Because, the way you repay something like that is to do it for the next one who needs it. Even if it's not the same people who did for you, and even if they didn't even live in the neighborhood during your personal crisis, you are still helping to keep the circle moving if you just try to be available as often as possible. And my parents were available often after we had received bountifully from the neighbors. Possibly even before this time.

I always remember riding down the street in the car when I was about 6 years old. A lady who lived at the end of our street was walking home from another neighbor's house, and waved us down in the middle of the street. She just walked out in the street and halted us. When she came to my mom's open car window, she told us how good "that lasagna" was. I was puzzled, and that stuck in my mind for years. First of all, how could lasagna be good? Or any other boring pasta barf? I hated when any of that was laid on me, and the later pasta fad of the '80's was like doing time for murder. Second, why did we send those guys lasagna? I thought it was a strange gesture – here you go, neighbor!

Many years later, (maybe about 20 or so), I asked about this incident. I didn't know if anyone would remember it, but it had been bugging me for a long time. I learned that this lady's mother had died at that time, and the circle was feeding the family for a few days. Oh, yeah, those guys! Circle 15. And so, you do pay it back in some way.

Often I would be at some neighbor's house while my mom was visiting with them, and had brought me along, being that I was too little to stay home alone. I would hear one of the neighbors going on about how they had so much to do in preparation for some event, and didn't know how they'd get it all done. Inevitably, someone would interrupt with the words, "I can do that!" or "I can do it!" It became a standard statement, an immediate and repeated volunteering of help.

And so I decided privately, "If everyone wants to 'do it' for everyone else, why not let them?" This applied, in my mind, to putting away my toys as well. I was not being a brat – I was letting them do what I thought they wanted.

Blame the good-hearted neighbors, not me. I was learning from example.

7. It Rolled off My Tongue

It was another case of learning from example. Being present at times when others got mad or annoyed, I often heard words that weren't meant for my ears. And some of the strongest words were accompanied by a fist being slammed on the nearest flat surface. Therefore, I associated a pound on the kitchen counter or a table, with certain words.

Back before the days when the rolls of refrigerated biscuits were made to open automatically after peeling the paper off the outside, a sharp rap on the edge of a table or counter was necessary to bust them open. I got used to seeing this early on, but often wondered why there was no yelling to help the process along.

I found out one day when I was about 4 years old. My mother had taken a roll of biscuits out of the refrigerator, and was about to prepare them for our breakfast. "Ah," I thought, "here's my chance to help her out!"

I sat at my place at the table, prepared for my role in the package opening process. And it came. I was poised, waiting for my turn to contribute, as she peeled off the outside paper. Almost time. And then came the crack of the roll on the counter.

"Damn!" the 4-year-old yelled, triumphantly and dutifully.

My mom looked up, startled. "Don't say that!" she said.

What was the problem? Just trying to help! I was truly baffled.

My oldest brother had had a similar experience to this one many years before. At that time, the family had a car that stalled easily. My mom had just learned to drive, and wasn't used to the temperamental nature of this vehicle. When the car would stall, my mom would smack the dashboard, and respond in a similar fashion to my later biscuit-making experience.

My brother had, in those same years, one of those toy carpenter's benches with the colored wooden pegs set into it, designed to be pounded from one side to the other with an accompanying wooden hammer. One day, my mom caught him on the floor, diligently pounding at each peg, and yelling, "Dammit! Dammit!" with each driving motion.

My mother asked him where he'd learned that. And the innocent answer from the small child was, "that's what you say, mommy!"

You'd think she would have learned by the time I showed up on the scene. Wonder where I picked it up? And could this be why they invented the rolls that pop open by themselves?

8. Color My Head Phitty

In my early years, my mother had a friend who lived down the street and one street over from us. She would often go to visit with her after my brothers and sister had gone to school. Because I wasn't in school yet, I was taken along.

This neighbor had a girl who was about 2 years behind me in age. She also had 6 other kids, but they were all in school before I was. There was probably a time when the second youngest was home while I was there – I do remember being with her, but I thought it was in the summer. Maybe it was during her kindergarten year, when she only had half a day at school. Or maybe I'm remembering some earlier times, before she started school.

In any case, most of my visits over there were spent with the youngest girl, Janie. Often, we would color in front of their fireplace, where the coloring books were scattered around haphazardly, at least once we got to them.

Janie had been taught to "color pretty". This meant keeping inside the black lines of the coloring book picture, rather than scribbling and going outside the lines. Each time we colored together, she had to keep her eye not only on her own picture, but mine as well. She was constantly telling me, "color phitty – stay inside the lines." I was, however, a scribbler, and my pictures always had jagged colored lines sticking outside their boundaries. She couldn't handle that.

Once, I accidentally did color something clearly inside the line, and she noticed. It was a picture of a drop of water falling on something, maybe a duck or a flower. I remember I colored the drop orange. Strange that she didn't comment on the color. Maybe she was used to rusty water - I didn't think so. But she suddenly exclaimed, "Hey, you stayed inside the lines on that!"

Well, I didn't mean to! But it looked so nice, I think I left it that way.

Most of the time, it annoyed me when she would correct me. I had gotten used to hearing, "color phitty", but that didn't mean I liked having her remind me all the time. Especially since she was a couple of years younger. Little snip of a shrimp, telling me what to do!

I'll always remember decking her in the living room one day. I don't know what brought it on – whether it was one more critique of my coloring skills or something else. And I don't think I meant to knock her down. I just gave her a push in exasperation over something. Just one little problem, though.

Crash! There was a footstool behind her, and she went backwards over it, landing partway on the floor on the other side of it with her legs still draped partway over the stool. The noise was disturbing enough to bring both of our mothers out of the kitchen where they'd been talking. I was stunned, not realizing I had exerted that much strength. She was dazed, having fallen suddenly backwards. I didn't know if she had hit her head or not. I was silently freaked out over having done this. I never did find out if she got a bruise or bump on her head.

Our mothers started questioning us as to what had happened. It should have been pretty clear that I was the one who had done the shoving. Considering that I was still standing and she was backwards on her rear on the other side of the footstool, I thought it was a bit self-explanatory.

Whether or not this whole thing had been started by her telling me for the hundredth time to "stay inside the lines", I'm still not sure, but I don't remember if she said that to me anymore after that day. She may have gotten the message, or maybe I just stopped listening so I wouldn't do something like that to her again.

A year or so later, after we had moved to California, my second grade teacher started giving us mimeographed pictures to color after we had finished our math worksheet each day. Yes, I said "mimeographed" as in purple ditto sheets – did I say I was young? Some of the students in my class were only in there for math. The school had worked out a system where some of the students would go into other rooms of the same grade during math class and some would stay in their own rooms. They kept me in my regular room, but the kid who sat in the desk attached to mine (who was also my next door neighbor at home), went into another class, and his seat was taken by a girl named Cathy from that room.

One day I noticed that Cathy had a unique way of coloring neatly. Without asking her if I could copy her method, I started doing it her way. She would first outline the picture with the crayon, pushing down hard to create a dark line. Then, when she would color the inside lightly, the outline of heavy wax also served as a barrier for stray marks. You could feel the crayon going up against the dark edge, and back off in time to keep inside the lines.

The school may have considered that we were wasting the crayons by doing that, but they never said anything. I was thrilled at the discovery of this technique Cathy used.

Too bad I wasn't still living near Janie so I could show her what I'd learned. I had finally picked up the skill of "coloring phitty", and she just might have been satisfied. As long as I didn't color her head phitty with the footstool.

9. Fanny in the Daytime – Monster at Night

As mentioned in my last book, it was a necessity of life in Kansas to have fans in the house in the summertime. And we had a bunch, as well as the air conditioner in the dining room. My brothers had small oscillating floor models, at least 2 if not 3 in their room. And we had two large window fans.

The window fan that was used in my parents' bedroom every summer was a large rectangle with beige blades and a small beige plate on the front in the center of the chrome-colored cage. This one always seemed tame to me. Something about it always reminded me of someone's grandma, gentle, smiling and cooing.

But the one in the room I shared with my sister was a terrifying monster. The blades inside the cage were a pale blue, which was soothing enough. But other than that, this fan had a scary face and a loud roar.

Sticking out of the front of the protective cage was a blue cylinder, matching in color to the blades. On the front of the cylinder was a single hole at the top, which looked like an eye in the middle of a head. Down below, the fan had been hit against something, forming a long horizontal dent. It looked like a big open mouth.

In the daytime, it wasn't quite as bad. The pale blue was a nice color, and the fan purred, just like the one I called Grandma. But at night, this fan would turn navy blue and roar. It scared the life out of me, sending me into nightly screaming fits.

In my very early years, when people would ask me why I was so scared of it, I would reply, "He opens he's eyes and he closes he's eyes!" It was the best I could do with my limited vocabulary at the time. Some would try to explain to me that the fan didn't have any eyes. To this, I would insist in frustration, "He goes," and then blink my eyes very hard and slowly, with emphasis, to get the point across.

I really don't remember seeing blinking eyes on this fan. I just knew about the single eye and the big mouth, ready to eat me up as soon as I fell asleep.

Because my sister was older, she often had the privilege of staying up later. I would be alone and defenseless in our double bed with this thing staring at me from across the room and roaring loudly. I would start calling for my sister, only to be met with my mother's voice calling back, "She'll be up in a little while!"

Great – and I'll be dead by then. She'll find my bones in bed, and a nasty fan licking its blue metallic lips.

Once we came home late in the evening, after dark. I don't know where we'd been; either a drive-in or at some function somewhere – maybe at our church at the end of the street. When I came into our bedroom, that thing was spinning furiously, now in its navy blue state and growling like a bear. My parents tried to get me to walk up to it and turn it off myself so I could see I had power over it, and it couldn't get me. I came close to doing it, but I still couldn't. It was too freaky. I think my dad turned it off, but I was terrified at how close I had gotten to it.

I tried to get over it at the time. Once, during the day, I told everyone the fan was my friend, and he had told me his name was Fanny. I would go up to pet it, listen to it purr, and enjoy its soft blue color. But that night, it was back to the same old monster, eerily whirring like a flying saucer.

I don't know if I ever got over the fear while we were still living there. After we moved to California, we didn't have as much of the stifling heat and humid summer weather as we did in Kansas. At least not until many years later. The fans were put away in the garage, and smaller models were used when needed.

My brother took the "Grandma" fan to some place of work where he was many years ago. It never came back home. I had thought it was the monster one that had been disposed of at that time, but one day my brother called me out to the garage to show me something. He told me to get up on the ladder he had set up, and look at what was on top of the storage cabinets. I've always had a fear of getting past the second step on a ladder, but I thought he had found something good. Instead, I found myself looking into the face of Fanny the Monster. By then, I was a teenager, and it didn't have the same effect on me as it had when I was a kid. But I knew my brother was teasing me. Creep!

The fan is still up on the cabinets, and I wonder if it still works. I may get it down soon and get a picture of it. Maybe I'll even plug it in and see what happens. I might even find out why or how, "He opens he's eyes and he closes he's eyes!" Then I can videotape it and send it to my brother – with instructions to play the tape at night with the sound way up.

10. Basement Games

Our basement in the house in Kansas had been set up as a playroom for us. We had a large toy box that my dad had built, which doubled as a giant bench. The bench seat had two large lids that could be lifted either from the top by a taller, stronger person or by the edge as we knelt on the floor in front of the box, preparing to search for toys inside.

Inside one lid was a section that had been left the full size, that is, half of the entire box. This was for larger sports items like baseball bats, badminton rackets, roller and ice skates, etc. Under the other lid of the box, that half had been separated into two compartments for smaller toys like dolls, Colorforms, blocks, and the like.

My mother was the Den Mother for the Cub Scouts while my brothers were members, and she held all of their meetings in the basement. A large piece of carpet, left over from the carpeting in the living and dining rooms upstairs, had been saved and put down in front of the toy box bench. This doubled as a wrestling mat for my brothers and a sitting place for the boys in the Cub Scout group when they would come. They would sit in a circle around its edge. I used to sit in on the Cub Scout meetings, and would usually go down there to play as I did any other time, but this time there was added entertainment. I got to listen to all of these rowdy boys acting up.

There was a Den Chief also, a boy who was about 5 or 6 years older than the Cub Scouts, and was in the school at the end of our street, connected with our church. All of the boys in the group were from that school as well.

Unfortunately, this boy who had volunteered as Den Chief was too busy still being one of the boys himself to be much help. Consequently, he did more harm than good in the group. I had always liked him, and didn't know until much later that my mother was less than thrilled with his presence, and ability to "help".

Still, I got a thrill out of listening to their antics. Once, my mom asked if anyone had a story to share. My brother, 2 years older than I, replied, "Once upon a time they lived happily ever after!" and dissolved in giggles immediately. My mom got annoyed and said, "Oh, come on!" She was trying to get some order and input in the meeting, and they weren't cooperating. Wonder why? Usually seven and eight-year-old boys are so accommodating!

Another time, she came into possession of a story, with blanks in the sentences. It was kind of like the Mad-Libs available commercially today, but long before their time. One difference was that instead of having people come up with their own words to put in the story, she made up cards with three words on each one. As she read the story to them, she would point at random to the various boys in the group whenever she reached a blank, and they would read one of the words on their list. Once the story got going, and became more and more nonsensical, the boys rocked on their heels, roaring in raucous laughter. I was enthralled.

Outside of Cub Scout meetings, there was a lot of other play that took place in the basement. One year at Christmas, my dad made us a ping pong table. I don't remember it being unfinished when we got it, but there are still pictures around that show four of us playing on a bare plywood table with no white lines marked. Later my dad painted it a nice rich green and put stripes of white on it, either by painting them between masking tape or using some kind of white tape. I had always thought it was tape because you could see the edges, but I didn't know at the time, how masking tape was used. It could have caused an edge when peeled off to reveal the higher white paint.

One corner of the basement had a spot of brown varnish or stain with newsprint in it. I was always fascinated by that, and wondered how the newspaper got printed on our basement floor. I don't remember it ever not being there, but I heard the story later about someone putting newspaper down when they were working on some sort of wood project and the varnish seeped through. I never knew if the paper got stuck and sealed to the floor or if the printing just transferred itself to the concrete by the dampness of the stain.

I had a life-sized black rubber mouse or rat with a squeaker in it, which I had requested on a shopping trip at some early time in my life. For some macabre reason, I used to place it on its side in that same corner of the basement and pretend it was dead. My game consisted mostly of warning people, "don't go over there! There's a dead mouse in the corner!" What a gross kid! Good thing I got over that!

Once, the Cub Scouts were working on some kind of wood project and there was a lot of sawdust around. I collected some, mixed it with water, put it in a tiny doll dish and called it "sawdust pudding". It was, I thought, a great recipe I'd invented. When I told one of the boys what it was, he made a face and stuck his tongue out. Some gourmet he was!

I also used to play church down there. We had a child size wooden bench of superior quality and design; I haven't seen one like it since. I think it might have started out in my brothers' room, but later made its way to the basement. I thought it looked like a church pew. I would sometimes move it over to one of the walls in the basement and face it toward the wall, where I would affix a large white and gold plastic crucifix that (I think) my brother had given me. The walls were cinder blocks, so there was no way I could drive a nail in, but I would use clay to stick the back of the cross to the wall. A two-by-four made a nice kneeler. I don't remember spending much time on the bench, but would sometimes go sit in front of the cross for a few minutes at a time. I left it up for awhile. Some kids played school; I played church. School came later, after we moved to California, and I set it up in my backyard, as we didn't have a basement.

One year, at Christmas, I got a playhouse, a stove, sink and refrigerator. The playhouse consisted of a frame made of metal rods that had to be assembled to form a cube with a peaked roof. The rods were then covered with a plastic sheet that had been fused at the edges into the shape of a house. The entire finished piece of plastic, which I believe had been pre-shaped by the manufacturer, would be slipped into place over the rod frame. There was a window cut in each of the side walls, maybe one in the front wall and a door in the front. I don't remember if the door was just a rectangular hole, or a flap like a tent would have. The outside of the house was printed with designs from the Mary Poppins movie, which was current at the time. I think it was made by Ideal or Hasbro, and there may have been other pictures printed on it to make it look like a house, like plants and shutters. I believe the plastic was pink with a red roof.

The kitchen appliances were real metal instead of plastic and were colored like some of the real ones; the coppery-brown enamel with a darker edge fading into the middle. I had thought these colors were more popular in the '70s, but I received these sometime in the mid-'60s, so the real ones must have come out earlier than I remembered.

These probably had to be assembled as well. Every parent's yearly Christmas nightmare!

The inside of the refrigerator door was printed with shelves full of food. There was an entire shelf of eggs removed from their carton, shelves of condiments, etc. I recognized the brand of mayonnaise they had in there. It was the brand sold in that part of the country, bearing a different name once we moved to California. It's the same brand my family has always used. I was thrilled to have it in my own refrigerator, even if it was only printed on.

The sink had a unique feature. On the back, behind the faucet area, was mounted a small oval pan. There was a hole in the backsplash of the sink, lining up with the faucet. The faucet was hollow and had a hole in the end, but I'm not sure if it was right in the end like a real faucet or if it ran across the end and opened on both sides. Because of its small size, they may have had to run the hole across to get it to flow properly. Maybe it even ran in both directions.

The oval reservoir in the back was to be filled with water. The faucet didn't automatically run, but if you moved it from side to side, or tapped it with a finger, you could get it to drip in the sink, or into a mini pot held under it. The only problem was that the metal used to build this appliance wasn't rust-proof, and after awhile, the reservoir was dark brown. I still kept it for a long time.

The backsplash behind the sink had been printed with a picture of tiles, a bar of soap in a dish, and maybe a scrub brush. It was all very realistic to me.

The stove had an oven underneath, and came with a set of red plastic pots and pans. Oh, and also a plastic turkey, which was one of my favorite pieces. The first day I had it I put the turkey in the biggest red pot and stuck it in the oven for Christmas dinner. It was not exactly the color of a raw turkey, but not like a cooked one either. It was kind of light yellow-tan, a little like a garbanzo bean. I may still have it.

We had an old wooden table with pockets built into the ends for holding magazines. It wasn't being used anymore, so it was given to me to use in my playhouse. My first grade teacher had asked us to bring in a piece of colorful oilcloth to place on our desks during art class, so we wouldn't mess things up. I went shopping with my mom, and got a piece with multi-colored tulips on it. I'm not sure if the background was red gingham or just a cream color. But the piece of fabric, because of the width that is generally sold, was cut in half. Half was taken to school and the other half became a tablecloth for my house.

Now I could really set up house. At some point, I decided I must be married, and chose the name "Stickhawk" as my last name. I don't even know where I got the word. Just made it up. I also didn't know that "Edna" wasn't a guy's name, so I decided privately that this was my husband's first name. I'm not sure where I had heard the name. Later, when I discovered on my own that this was a female given name, I settled for "Ed". Nobody else knew about it anyway, so I didn't have to deal with having anyone laugh at me.

One evening, I decided that people were coming over, and needed to know where my house was. I made up a small sign that said, "Theresa Stickhawk" and put it in a front window. Later, I showed it to my mom, and she was puzzled. She didn't know what it meant, and no way was I going to explain it to her. I ended up throwing it away.

When we moved to California the next year, we didn't have a basement. With few or no tornadoes, there was no need for a place to hide out until the storm passed. Only the older houses had cellars, and our house had been freshly built. Somehow we thought the weather would be tame enough to set up the playhouse in the back yard. But the first winter we were here, it rained heavily and constantly, and the wind was too much for the thin plastic. The outside of the house blew off and tore, and the rod frame twisted out of shape.

For some reason, instead of throwing the whole thing in the trash, we burned the plastic part in the fireplace. My parents let me watch, as the plastic turned all kinds of neat colors in the heat. This show of color was supposed to make up for my losing my house.

Nobody thought about what the plastic fumes might have been doing to our lungs and sinuses, or the air in the neighborhood, as they went out the chimney. All I knew is that Mary Poppins went up the chimney in a blaze, (literally), never to return.

11. Poison Ivy, Grass Stains, Mushrooms, and Other Strange Things

Just as a duckling, opening his eyes for the first time will follow the first creature he sees, supposing it's his mother, there are many instances that come to mind where I associated what I saw with what was happening at the time. And it took me awhile to realize there was no connection.

Do you know that there was a time when I really believed cats gave you grass stains? I had always been told it wasn't a good idea for a kid to have white pants. Someone who spends most of his or her time playing should have something that doesn't reveal everything that gets dropped, smeared or squirted on it. But I did have white pants more than once in my life.

The people who lived next door to us had a white cat named Johnny White. The cat received his name after the kid up the street got a brown dog and named it after the man next door to us, giving the dog the name Charlie Brown. Where else have I heard that name? It may not have been too original, but this kid seemed to admire my next door neighbor, and the dog's name stuck. Shortly after, the family next door got a white cat, and knew just what to name him. The kid was reciprocated in kind.

One day, I was outside, and Johnny White had been let out to explore the area. I was a bit afraid of cats then; I may have been told scary stories by the males in my household who have all hated cats from the beginning. Or I may have already gotten the "cat got your tongue?" line laid on me a few times too many. Maybe it was just that I had noticed how sneaky they acted while hunting prey and that could look creepy to a kid. In any case, I didn't want to hang around when I saw Johnny White coming my way. I got up, ran, fell and skidded through the grass in my long white pants.

When I got up, there was a strange green spot on the knees of my pants. What did that cat do to me? I didn't know anything about grass stains at the time, and I was sure he had inflicted something strange on my clothes.

Another time, I was swinging on our backyard swing set, which was the old-fashioned kind with the chain links on each of the swings. When I jumped off the swing into the grass, two of the links smashed together, pinching my little finger and drawing a couple small drops of blood.

And, as I landed on my feet in the grass, the first thing I saw was a tiny patch of mushrooms! I had heard of poisonous mushrooms. Could they, I wondered, have anything to do with my pinching my finger in the chain? Maybe they had squirted their poison at me, causing me to slip as I jumped. I didn't know cats and mushrooms had such powerful talents.

As mentioned numerous times in this book, the things I heard could be misunderstood in the same way as the things I saw. In Kansas, there was poison ivy around, something I haven't seen in California, but we more than make up for it with poison oak. At an early age, I was told that if I ever saw poison ivy, "Don't go near it."

Therefore, I really thought this plant had the ability to "throw" its poison at people. If it was just that I wasn't supposed to come in contact with it, wouldn't they have said, "Don't touch it"? I didn't know that they just wanted to ensure that I didn't come close enough to brush up against it. If I didn't go near it, there was less chance of doing that.

I did hear later that it is possible for the wind to blow some of the poison off, and therefore this was another reason not to be too close. But that wasn't what I had in mind when I gave myself a good ten or twenty foot distance from the plants.

And, there were the watermelons. This is a slightly different sort of thing, but another "Kiddie Perception" I had that came from what I was seeing and what I had seen in the past. Every year, my family would go camping for a week or so at a place called "Roaring River". We spent a lot of time cooling in the river, as the Midwestern summers were hot and nasty. Often I would see watermelons floating on the other side of the river and believed for years that people had put them there as markers to swim to.

There was a big public swimming pool near our home that we went to every night during the summer. My mom would get dinner ready early; we'd all get into our swimming suits and wait for my dad to come home. When he got there, he'd change into his swimming trunks immediately and we'd all leave for the pool. After swimming for awhile, we'd head home for the dinner that was ready and waiting for us.

The pool had the usual ropes with the blue and white bobbers on them to separate the deep end from the shallow. My mom would sometimes let me ride on her back like a baby koala, and she'd walk to the rope where I could touch one of those oval eggs. Others would use these ropes as places to swim to, maybe swimming underwater to the deep end. I couldn't swim yet, but I always liked touching those things.

So, I figured, a lake or river doesn't have ropes in it like that, so people had to find something that would float slightly so they could see it to swim to. What could work better than bobbing watermelons?

It was years before I was told that this was a popular method for cooling the watermelons so they could be eaten. I don't know if I had considered asking at the time, and I don't think anyone explained it to me. I probably learned the truth years later when I mentioned this unique "water game".

12. What Comes After Wednesday?

You do tend to wonder what people are listening to, when you discover that you can run through the house yelling something, and nobody remembers it later. In my case, this happened several times that I can think of.

Though my parents claim that they taught me all of the basic stuff that is taught to kids before starting school, I swear I never heard of Thursday before kindergarten. As if in compensation for this, I didn't fully learn to tell time until fifth grade, and that was finally set in place at home. This was taught in school, but I had a very hard time grasping the concept. The math teacher I had in third grade was a little spacey, and a lot of people seemed to have a hard time understanding her teaching practices. Often, when I would be alone with her in the classroom, or standing near her desk, she would ask me, "What time is it?" just to see if I'd picked it up yet. I could never answer her, and be sure I was right. It would be a couple of years before the final nail was driven into my head on this issue. I never knew why it took me so long to get this.

But in the case of learning the days of the week, you would think someone would have picked up early in the game that I was skipping one. For, as a source of time-passing amusement, I would often run through the living room chanting, "SaturDAY, SunDAY, MonDAY, TuesDAY, WednesDAY, FRI-I-I-day!" Once I would reach the end, I would start over, as if reciting a mantra or doing a rain dance. You had to get the rhythm just right.

How was it that they didn't notice that? Maybe it had something to do with the fact that I was kid number five, and they were used to chatter enough to block out the background stuff like that. But, if I remember correctly, I was LOUD when I did this…also, persistent, and repetitious.

There was another chant of this type that I did later, and I don't remember anyone asking me about this one either. I had become interested in cars when I was about 5 or 6, and had learned to identify several models. My next door neighbor had a Pontiac GTO, which was either black or navy blue. I think it was black. I didn't see many of those around, so I was fascinated whenever I did spot the real thing on the road. There were times when I thought I was seeing one, but the only marking I could find on it was on the back, where it said Bonneville. I never did find out who made that model. I would always have to check the front grille to see if there was a large GTO embedded in there. There usually wasn't.

One day, my brothers and I were in the garage of this same neighbor, and he was giving stuff away that he thought would be fun for us to have. He had old license plates, for this was a time and place where you would get a new one every year, and have to replace it on your car. Some people kept the old ones as decorative souvenirs, and had them hanging in their garages, basements, recreation rooms or bedrooms. My brothers received a few of these from this neighbor, and hung them on their bedroom walls.

This man then came across some small note pads with leather or faux leather covers. I never did know what kind of work he did. These covers had gold initials stamped in them, and I never knew if they were samples from a printing company or if the initials belonged to people who hadn't shown up for a meeting. He gave us each one. I don't remember the initials of the ones my brothers got, but mine said, "GTW". Being into cars at that time, I immediately recognized the similarity between my book's initials and the car owned by the man who gave these to us.

So I had something new to yell. For the longest time after receiving this note pad, I found myself dashing around, chanting, "GTW and GTO!" I couldn't get enough of it. There are still times when that one comes into my head for no apparent reason, and I have the urge to yell it repeatedly. Ironic, after all these years!

I still wonder why I was never questioned about either of these things. It does explain, however, why the weekends seem to take so long to get here.

Okay, so what comes after Wednesday?

13. The Unsolved Mysteries of the Boxer and the Horse

In all these years, I still haven't figured this one out. Hallucinations? Dreams? Bad drugs for my many bladder infections? I may never know what happened.

Two instances come to mind of times when I clearly saw something that didn't make sense. One was out in the front yard in Kansas. The other was in my parents' bedroom, and I believe it was after we had moved to California.

I was scared to death of dogs when I was a kid. Maybe it was because of the one down the street who used to chase running kids for fun, thinking they were playing, and wanting to get in on it. Trouble was he scared most of the kids, who assumed he was looking for a bite of fresh meat off of them.

Also, the dog next door was known to have bitten a few people. He almost got my dad one night when the neighbors' gate had been left open and the dog had gotten loose. He was known to growl at us in our own backyard, and jump up to hug the top of the fence, threatening to go over. One of his owners, a kid that I sometimes played with, but was often tormented by, knew I was afraid of the dog, and would sometimes open his gate and yell for his pet, throwing me a sadistic grin. Why I continued to play with him is beyond me.

I had also witnessed my brother being bitten on the butt by a terrier in the neighborhood one day. He had been playing hide-and-seek with some other kids in the area, and I had tagged along from afar to see what was going on. This dog was tied up in his backyard, which the kids were running through as if it were their own. I never did find out who owned that house or that dog.

It was my brother's turn to hide his eyes and count as the others hid. But he had to go to the bathroom in the middle of it all, so he told them he'd go home and come back later to find them. I stayed standing in the next yard over from this dog, watching him staring at me, but being beyond the length of his rope.

I saw a group of kids running through the yard and peeking around a corner to see if my brother was coming back yet. They saw that the coast was clear, and ran off somewhere else after whispering to each other.

A few minutes later, my brother came romping back. As he galloped past the terrier, the dog leapt out and bit him on the rump. Others seemed to notice, and the game was stopped. I ran home from there, and I think my other brother was behind me, ready to convey the news to my mom when we got in the house. He did, before I could.

"Barry got bit by a dog!" my brother said, and my mom went out to find him. I think he was almost home by then, and my mom checked him out in the bedroom. He had an open red line, a cut which I saw that evening when she displayed it for my dad. I don't remember if he got any kind of treatment for it; they certainly couldn't bill the dog's owner since my brother was trespassing on their property. But they may have checked with the owners to see if the dog was up to date on his shots. Otherwise, that canine was only doing his job of protecting his property.

Some time later, I heard of a family who had a white goose in a pen in their backyard. I think the owner may have been a friend of my oldest brother, and they may have said we could come over to look at the goose. We discovered that if we ran through the side yard of the people across the street, and went straight through their backyard, we would wind up in the backyard of the people with the goose. It was a shortcut that even I could memorize, and I've always gotten lost easily. The first few times, I was with my brothers when we'd visit the goose, but one day I decided to venture forth by myself.

There I was, standing by the pen, checking out the big bird, when I suddenly looked up and into the yard behind this family's house. I was being watched. And it was *the dog*. I recognized the square, hairy face. It was the same one that had made rear contact with my brother.

I ran out of that yard faster than I can ever remember running at any other time. I never went back to see the goose.

So I did have a lot of reasons to fear dogs. Any time I would see one anywhere, I would scream and run, often annoying the owners who sneered at me in disgust over being such a baby.

And then there was the day I saw the boxer. Not a guy in shorts, putting up his dukes, but a dog. I was lying in the front yard, doing nothing, just vegging in the grass. All of a sudden, a dog the size of a horse ran by, leaping somewhat gracefully like a deer or a galloping horse. I knew it was a boxer; my friend Margie had one of those. But how did it get so big? They were big, but not like that! As I looked around, fathoming where this beast came from, it was suddenly gone. I still don't know what happened. Had I fallen asleep in the Kansas sun?

Then there was the horse. This time was a couple of years later, after we had moved to California. And this is something that must have been a dream. There's no other explanation, unless I was on hard drugs, and at age 7 or 8 I wasn't. Nor was I most of my life, unless something was forced on me, or if you count having to smell pot fumes emanating from my brother's room. I must have fallen asleep this time.

On Saturday mornings, when my dad was still working, (long before retirement age, that is,) he would often sleep in a little later. He usually got up around 5 a.m. on weekdays to catch the train to work, but on Saturdays he would stay in bed until 9 or 10. My mom would be up early and reading the newspaper or working downstairs, so I would sometimes climb in bed with my dad for a few minutes. Nothing kinky, like you might hear about today; just a little time with the parent who wasn't home as much as the other one. He'd reach for my hand, hold on gently and snooze off and on, content.

After awhile, I'd get bored and try to leave. He'd wake up, act betrayed in a teasing way, and say, "you gonna leave me?" I'd get guilt-tripped and stay a little longer. After about 3 attempts, I'd finally go anyway – I was too bored watching him sleep, and besides, I hadn't had breakfast yet.

One morning I was lying on my mom's side of the bed, sure I was awake, and I looked over at their dresser. And there, right in the middle on the front of the dresser, between the two sets of drawers was a horse's head! It didn't look real enough to be something out of "The Godfather" - rather it looked something like Pokey on the Gumby show. I think its tongue was hanging out. It was only there for a second or two and then disappeared. But it was so real, and I "knew" I hadn't fallen asleep.

How can something so real be a dream? Considering that I was petrified of dogs at that time, I suppose that thought was tucked away in my mind at all times, and could have come out in any dream. That event could have been real, however, even with the dog being that big. I was, after all, about six years old at the time, so anything could have looked bigger than it really was. I remember going back to the neighborhood years later and discovering that things were closer together than they had been and a lot of things were smaller. Had they moved and shrunk? No, my legs were longer and I was bigger. The only thing that makes me think the dog was a dream is the fact that it disappeared from sight so fast. And it was easy to fall asleep outside in the summertime.

The horse, however, had to have been a dream. I've *never* been on that kind of drugs.

14. Back in the Dogwood House Again

In my early years, before I was in school, and also during my kindergarten year when I was home in the mornings, my mom would often go to visit with one or the other of the neighbor ladies. Sometimes it would be a lady who lived down the street and over one street from us. Other times it would be the lady next door or a lady who lived around the bend from us (who turned out to be my aunt's aunt, though I didn't find that out for years).

The visits would consist of lots of talking and lots of coffee. Being a kid, I would often get bored, except when I would be able to pet the cat next door. Her name was Puddyfoot, and she was the one who I had first noticed had a mustache. But she didn't always stick around to entertain a little kid, even though she had some in her own house. Or maybe it was because she had some in her own house, and was used to being harassed! I do remember petting her once when she was reclining on her side in a sunbeam in the window.

I had always been taught not to pick other peoples' flowers, unless they were dandelions, which most people would be happy to get rid of. This had been instilled in me early on. This is why I was puzzled one day when my mom made a suggestion to me to relieve my boredom.

We were in the next door neighbors' living room, and had been there for some time; at least it seemed so to me, being a kid. My mom could see I was getting restless, and suddenly gave me an idea for something to do.

"Why don't you go out and pick some flowers?" she said.

Since we were in this other family's house, I assumed she was referring to the blossoms of the dogwood tree out in their front yard. Why was I suddenly given permission to do this? I figured she had made the suggestion with the idea that the neighbor lady could object if she didn't want me to do it. I ventured outside to the dogwood tree.

I didn't want to overdo my privilege, so I only picked four. They were large, floppy blossoms, so I thought I could make do with a small amount, and make it seem like a lot.

I came back in the house a little later with the giant flowers drooping over my small hand. My mom saw what I had and was slightly surprised and apologetic, explaining only then what she had really meant.

Turned out she'd been talking about the lilies-of-the-valley, which grew along the side of our own house, close to the wall on this neighbor's side. This house we were visiting in was the house that Kris (mentioned in the next chapter and in my last book), lived in later, but the old neighbors hadn't moved at this time. Picking the delicate, bobbing bells of the lilies-of-the-valley by our own house had always been a luxurious pastime for my sister and I, when we were allowed.

There was nothing I could do for those four dogwood blossoms by then, and I believed my neighbor understood. She had three kids of her own. But I think I may have been given clearer instructions after that!

15. The Crabby Apple Dog

At the age of 6, I often played with the kid next door, an older boy of 10 named Kris. He was mentioned in my last book. Yeah, the mischievous tyrant who almost sent me to my demise, down the concrete steps in my wagon. I never knew when he might go off and play some nasty trick to get out of playing with me. And I don't think they made bike helmets back then.

And when we would be playing, and he wanted to stop, he could never tell me that. He always had to devise some way to ditch me.

One of our pastimes consisted of tormenting a certain neighborhood dog we had discovered living in the house behind the place next door to me. Not the house Kris lived in, but on the other side of me. The yards that did have fences in that neighborhood, had the chain-link variety, so it was easy to see into other peoples' yards, and go into the yards that didn't have fences around them.

I was normally scared to death of dogs back then, but when I knew one was behind a fence and didn't have a way out, especially a very small dog that couldn't jump over, I would sometimes go right up to the fence to see it. Kris and I had discovered that this dog was one of the very nervous, yappy sorts, who couldn't stand not being able to get out and rip us up. Perfect for our tantalizing purposes! We were unrelenting in our nastiness with this animal.

One of our other neighbors, the family on the other side of Kris, had a crab apple tree in their front yard. It was abundant with fruit in season, and was a source of simple-minded amusement for a lot of kids in the neighborhood. One of the favorite pastimes of a lot of kids was to pick up a crab apple that had fallen off this tree, and use it to draw on the sidewalk. After breaking the apple's skin, you could get a nice thick line by rubbing the pulp on the concrete, drawing pictures, writing messages or just scribbling. The lines darkened after awhile, as any apple will when it comes in contact with the air.

At first, when Kris and I started bugging this dog, we would just jump around and make noise on the other side of the fence, antagonizing him into a frenzied barking. I'm not sure how long this went on before we graduated to the practice of throwing crab apples through the fence at him. That really got him mad, and amused us greatly, sadistic little brats that we were.

Sometimes, when we would be playing together, we would become bored and try to think of what to do next. Inevitably, Kris's face would light up suddenly, and he would say in his somewhat garbled way, "Hey, let's go see that dog!"

I was always willing to accommodate. We would take off running, across my front lawn, through my side yard, partway across my next-door neighbors' back yard and ending at the fence. Sometimes the dog was out in his yard, sometimes he wasn't. We had to take the chance of possibly being disappointed that we couldn't harass him this time around.

I was at the dentist's office once, and after my appointment was over, the dentist let me pick something out of his prize chest. I couldn't decide between a hard plastic metallic red double bed charm, molded in detail with a quilt, or a small soft plastic red toy lunch box. They let me take both. The bed was about the size of a quarter or a little smaller, and the lunch box was a little bigger. I carried them around for awhile, and kept opening and closing the lid on the lunch box.

Alas, I didn't have the lunch box long. I think I had the bed for some time after that, but the lunch box met its demise in the mouth of the nasty little dog on one of my annoyance missions. I don't remember if I was with

Kris or went over by myself to torment the football-sized canine, but I was carrying my treasures. The lunchbox fell inside the chain-link fence, too far to reach in without the dog noticing. I tried briefly to get my hand in and quickly retrieve the item, but the dog reacted with heavy snarling as he headed for the fleshy tidbit that housed my fingernails. I pulled my hand out just in time. The dog, not happy about missing my hand, immediately went for the soft plastic toy and chewed it for a short time before dropping the holey mass of red stuff.

One day, Kris decided he didn't want to play with me anymore, and told me he had to go to the bathroom. He went into his house, and I waited for him. A few minutes later, I was in my backyard, and saw him coming out his back door into his own yard. He looked happy and carefree, as if he'd just gotten out of doing some grueling chore. I thought he must have had to hit the bathroom really bad!

When he didn't come right over, as I had expected, I went back and knocked on his front door. His brother answered, and went to get Kris. Kris came out, but was annoyed that I hadn't gotten the message. He sat on the front step dejectedly, complaining, "Why'd you have to come over and call for me? I knew you'd have to come over and call for me!"

I was surprised, but I'm not sure if I agreed to go home at that time, or stayed and forced him to be with me. But I do know there were other times when he was more blunt and up-front about it. One time comes to mind, as he tricked me into leaving his house when we were playing inside.

Kris was bored again, but as usual, couldn't ask me to leave. So, as in other instances, his face brightened with the verbally expressed idea, "Hey, let's go see that dog!"

I bit the bait. "Yeah, an' throw crab apples at him!"

Kris opened his front door and allowed me to go out first. Then, after I was completely out on the doorstep, he stepped back inside and slammed the door, leaving me out there alone, surprised and baffled.

Well, at least the dog was happy that day!

16. Washing My Own Mouth with Soap

Another event at Kris' house – this time was one of the rare days when we played inside his house. A game I had learned from one of my brothers was an alternative version of hide-and-seek. However, instead of hiding yourself, one person would cover his eyes, and the other would hide an object or group of objects.

I had brought over a bunch of soaps; the tiny guest soaps that usually come in a gift box, either in an assortment of colors and/or shapes, or in with other bath items like bubble bath or a body scrubber of some sort. I think these soaps had been given to me by a neighbor who lived across the street. They were all round, about the size of a nickel, and were all in different colors, about five or six of them. Kris and I took turns hiding them, and letting the other look for them.

I don't remember how many "rounds" we did each. But I do believe that this took place either on a Saturday or Sunday. The reason being, Kris' dad was home from work that day.

At one point, when it came my turn to hide them, Mr. Varney motioned for me to hide one in his hand, which he would keep casually closed. Kris would never think of looking there. Somehow, I remember vaguely, that the pink one was the one that I put in his hand.

And he was right – that Kris would never check his father's hand for the soap. Long after he'd found the others, and couldn't think of any other place to look, Kris gave up searching and wanted to quit the game.

…Which was just as well, because I was getting bored and decided I wanted to go home. There was one little problem, though. Mr. Varney still had my pink soap, and he was fast asleep in his chair now! What was I going to do? In those days, I didn't talk to many adults in the neighborhood, only 4 that I can think of, and he wasn't one of them. Besides, he was snoozing away! I had been taught enough about respecting adults at that time that I really didn't want to bother him. This was, after all, one of his days off from work, and he clearly needed to rest. How could I get my soap back?

I suppose I could have just left it there, and asked Kris for it the next time I saw him. I didn't think of it, though. Being 6 years old, I was mainly concerned with recovering my possession as quickly as possible. And this is where my respect for adults waned a bit.

I decided, after much quiet deliberation, that the best way to wake him up and make him drop the soap at the same time would be to, ever so gently, bite his hand. After weighing the idea, and trembling inwardly for a short time, I finally went over to where he was sitting, got up close to his big hairy hand and nipped him lightly.

"AAARRRGGGHH!" Mr. Varney growled loudly, dropping my hand-cleansing agent. I don't know if he was mad, surprised or hurt, but I made my getaway quickly, pink soap in hand with the others. You might say I made a clean break.

I hope he figured it out once he was fully awake. I don't remember ever being questioned about the incident.

17. River of Syrup, Pool of BBQ Sauce

When we lived in Kansas, and most of our relatives were in Missouri, much of our vacation time was spent in St. Louis. Though we were on the Missouri side of Kansas, it was still a long drive, especially for 5 kids. We were often asking how much farther we had to go. Therefore, there were a lot of games and pastimes devised to make it seem faster, or at least more interesting. Usually the suggestions to "look at the cows" didn't hold our attention very long, but sometimes would suffice for a few seconds, anyway. But it took more than that to keep us up and interested.

One game we played was "Sticky Stuckey's". I'm not sure who started this, but there was some establishment, a restaurant or motel or something that was called "Stuckey's". They had a bunch of large billboards along the road, which were yellow with red script, spelling out the name of the place. I think it was a restaurant; yellow and red seem to be used a lot on signs for places like coffee shops and fast food joints. It seemed fitting. It may have been both, however.

Some family member started the tradition of yelling, "Sticky Stuckey's!" every time we'd come upon one of these signs, indicating the number of miles to the place. We did it on each trip, for as far back as I can remember.

We also had names for certain kinds of cars, which I think, one of the neighbor boys may have informed my brothers about. The original game was just counting Volkswagens, which were, for some reason, named Beavers. I had thought the neighbor made this up, but years later, a friend of mine from fifth grade told me she had heard of it. Only, in her case, the term, "beaver" only referred to a certain model of Volkswagen. She told me a bunch of other names for the other models of this brand, but I've forgotten them.

After awhile, my family wasn't satisfied with only counting Volkswagens, and some of us made up names for other types of cars. I came up with "There's One" for Corvairs, "Thing" for a certain model of van which was sometimes used for school buses or telephone company trucks, (I never was sure of the make), "Monster" for Ford Galaxies, (because my aunt had an accident in hers, named it "that monster" and never drove again), "GTO" for Pontiac GTO's, (original, huh?), and others. My sister called sports cars "fairies", which prompted me to call very large cars "elephants". My brother decided Ford Mustangs would be called "horses". I also decided on certain combinations, which had to be seen and called in the order I set them up. I don't know if anybody ever joined me in this more complex form of the game. The two combinations I came up with were, "Horse, Beaver, There's One", "Beaver, GTO, There's One, There's One" and later, "Monster, Beaver, There's One"

Another game I came up with, which remained mine alone, was claiming to spot pancakes floating in the Missouri River. Each time we would cross that area, I would look out the window and say, "I see the pancakes!"

I'm not sure how this started. I do know that in my early days when I would take baths with my sister, we used to sometimes make flowers out of our washcloths and give them to each other to smell (hopefully before we had used them). We would do this by laying the washcloth out flat on the surface of the water and quickly putting one fist under it before it could sink. After lifting the part with the fist in it out of the water, we'd then use the free hand to grab all of the edges of the washcloth together and pull out the fist. This would cause a giant air bubble in the washcloth, with the bottom bunched tightly together in one hand. The free hand that had been the fist was now used to smash the bubble into a flat round. I always liked the fizzy sound the air made coming through the weave of the washcloth fabric as we each smashed ours down. Then, the index finger would be used to poke a center in the flower.

It seems that there was one evening when I decided to make pancakes out of my washcloth instead of flowers. I don't know if this came about before or after the Missouri River fantasy. But I did somehow make the connection.

I halfway remember that someone used to mention bottles floating in the river. There was some talk about the bottles having messages in them for someone to open up and read, but I don't remember if these were the same bottles in the river, or if that was part of some other story, something like Gilligan's Island. But I decided at some point that they were probably syrup bottles, and there must be pancakes floating somewhere in the river to go with them. Maybe this was because the river was so brown. I've never been sure.

...Rivers of syrup...that brings to mind another incident. In Kansas, and possibly Missouri, the grocery stores carried a brand of barbecue sauce that I haven't seen in stores in California. It came in a large bottle, especially large for a kid to handle with small hands. When we used this at the table, I usually had to have it, (and my milk from the half-gallon carton) poured by an adult. There was a reason for this.

One night, at the table, I picked up the barbecue sauce bottle, apparently thinking that maybe I had finally gotten big enough to handle it. Either that or I was impatient and didn't want to wait for someone else to be available to pour it. I can't imagine that, though - I was always the model of patience! Yeah, right, whatever. As a result of my adventurous spirit, though, I ended up pouring myself a plateful of the spicy red-brown stuff.

For the rest of the meal, everybody else was dipping their meat in my plate instead of pouring their own. I hated it, but we couldn't waste half a bottle! It drove me nuts, having to dodge everybody else's arms and forks for the whole meal. You know, there are spoons you could use to get some of this out of my plate and onto your own! Nobody thought of it at the time.

Years later, when I went back to visit my old neighborhood, I was in a grocery store and saw these big bottles of barbecue sauce. I had almost forgotten about them. Somehow, the bottles had gotten a little smaller over the years, though!

I bought one to take home for old memories. And this time, at age 20, my hand was big enough to prevent a flood.

One question, though. Just who *is* Barbara Q. Soss?

18. Grandpa's House

One of the big deals about going to St. Louis several times a year was staying at my Grandpa's house. He had extra bedrooms in a great old brick house which we had wonderful times hanging out in. Somehow I always got stuck sleeping in the crib upstairs, even after I was older. I think it may have been the only choice. The older ones got first pick of the real beds, and that's all that was left for me.

On one of these trips, I discovered that I had forgotten my doll, a blonde baby named Kathy, who I had had for years, and slept with nightly. That's when my mom invented a Kleenex doll for me to substitute for Kathy, at least until we got home. For years after that, I often had her make me these dolls, which didn't last too long since I slept with them and shredded their tissue bodies, but were easy enough to make fresh each day. I've considered making one recently, just to see if I can remember how. I don't know that I've ever tried, but I watched my mom often enough.

I remember getting to my grandpa's one night after dark, and all of us standing on the front porch, knocking to see if he'd answer. My dad finally used his key, and I think we discovered my grandpa was in the shower. My sister had gotten a wild wig for Christmas that year, and someone mentioned playfully that she should wear it in the house and see what my grandpa would do. That was the first time I heard anyone use the phrase, "he might jump out of his skin". It was decided quickly she shouldn't do that, especially if he happened to be getting out of the shower.

He had a fancy house; not only was it made of brick, it had an arch-shaped front door which I always found quaint. There was a cast iron brace on the chimney; all of the others in the area had them, but this one was a completely different shape. Rather than being "S" shaped like most, it was more like a bracket used in punctuation, with added curlicues at each end. The kitchen floor had a design in the linoleum tiles with different colored squares in a pattern among the white or off-white ones. I used to try to jump from one colored set to the other, but they were too far apart for my short legs. There were also the ceramic tiles characteristic of many old houses, which were one color for the main part and another for the borders and the narrow stripe in the wall above the counter. I don't remember these from his house, but years later when I saw them in someone else's old house, I was told they had been in my grandpa's house as well. I wished then that I'd kept a mental picture of them, especially in the upstairs bathroom, where I'm told they were purple and turquoise. I got a picture of the outside of this house in 1981, but it would have been nice if the owners had let us go inside as well. Nobody wanted to knock on the door and ask.

At least, by 1981, the black dog next door would have been gone. I always remember this little curly-haired football – some sort of poodle or poodle-mix. My sister reported being chased by it a number of times, and I think I was once also. The landscaping around the house was hilly, and this dog was often out loose by himself. I was in the backyard once, and suddenly remembered being warned about this dog. I think I may have run around to the front even though there was a back porch there. I don't remember if I just got myself worked up over nothing, or if I really did spot the dog at the last second as I slammed the front door.

Other things to remember at his house were the fan, the green ottoman and the picture behind the sofa. Also, the one time he let me "color" pictures in the newspaper. I'll go over each of these in detail separately.

The electric window fan on my grandpa's indoor back porch was already described in detail in the earlier chapter entitled, "Fanny in the Daytime, Monster at Night". This one was exactly the same as his, right down to the dent that formed the "mouth" of this creature. I don't remember ever seeing his fan turned on, so I wasn't as afraid of his as I was of ours. Also, ours was always more scary at night, and the room I slept in at his house was upstairs, away from the porch. So it was just a matter of having to look at it from afar, and wonder how it followed us to St. Louis. The truth was my grandpa gave us the one we had. I don't know how they both managed to get dented in the same place, though.

His ottoman, which he had in his living room, was covered in a medium-dark green, fake leather upholstery material. What I always remembered about it was the patch in the corner, on the top surface. It seemed to be fashioned from black electrical tape, or maybe it was a tire patch. It always reminded me of the devil's food cookies we used to buy. They were two layers of cake, separated by a thin layer of white cream, and the whole thing dipped in chocolate. They looked like miniature sofa pillows, because they tapered down at the edges rather than having flat sides. The cookies, and especially the frosting, were dark brown and the patch on the ottoman was black, but it still reminded me of these cookies.

There was a picture behind his sofa, which was probably a print of a famous painting, but I didn't know at the time what it was called. I just remember a girl in a red blouse and golden skirt, (or perhaps it was a dress in those colors), holding a white cat, which was draped in her arms and hanging down. I remember looking at this, as I would lie on his sofa. Years later, I found out it was called, "Chums" by Jane Freeman, and was able to acquire a small, framed print of it.

Once, I was looking for some pictures to color, and my grandpa didn't have such a thing as a coloring book in his house. He gave me ads from the newspaper that had pictures of women modeling clothes, and said I could color them. All I had was a pencil, for he had no crayons there either. I was a bit limited on what I could color, for a black-and-white photo already has areas that are the same color as a regular pencil. For some reason, I took delight in penciling in mustaches on all of the women. Once I had done it with all of the women in one ad, I would move on to the next. My grandpa was puzzled. "Don't you want to color them?" he'd ask repeatedly. I would point to what I had done, but he didn't seem to understand.

His wife had died when I was a year old, so I didn't remember being with her in that house, or anywhere else. I've only seen one picture of her; in my parents' wedding pictures. But I do remember those vacations, which were divided mostly between his house and my other grandparents' house, detailed slightly in the next chapter. A great time was had by all.

19. Grandma's Toy Drawer

Another place we visited in St. Louis was the home of my other grandparents. This was in another area of town, a small house I remember having stones set into the concrete in the front wall. I remember arriving there and having my grandma wave to us, as she had been standing on the porch waiting for us. Time for more good times!

My aunt had never married, and lived with her parents up until they died. She had a steady job and contributed much to the family income. She was always an added bonus to the visits to their house, and took care of my grandparents until the end of their lives, later arranging for their funerals, selling their house and moving herself into several apartments over the years. We looked forward to seeing all three of them at that house when we came several times each year.

One major star attraction at Grandma's house was the toy drawer, which we had all become familiar with at an early age. It was the bottom drawer in a piece of furniture in their dining room; I'm not even sure what else the furniture held. It may have been a breakfront of sorts, or a china cabinet. It almost seems as if it might have been a desk. I do remember some piece of furniture on that same wall that had a row of solid-colored cups sitting on top, each a different color. They were somewhat small and unusual shaped; I don't think I would have picked them for drinking out of since I'm into big drinks, but I always thought they looked nice. That may have been the contention of others as well, since I never saw them taken down. I'm not sure if these were on the same piece of furniture that had the toy drawer.

But we all knew we were allowed to head there right away. In this drawer was always a stuffed bear that came from the St. Louis zoo. It was a black bear with a flesh-colored plastic muzzle, painted or printed with brown whiskers and nose. Around its neck was a red plastic collar with a buckle and attached to this was a metal chain leash with a red loop. This item was to stay there at all times, but sometimes the smaller items would wind up going home with us. We never knew what would be in there from one time to the next.

The milk bottles at that time, had a plastic disc for a lid, and in order to entice kids to collect them and drink more milk, they had pictures of baseball players on them. There would usually be some of those in the drawer, and my brothers would be told about them ahead of time so they could check them out and see if they had any of the guys on them. At least, I think it was baseball. I always hated sports, so I never looked real closely at them. Baseball and football especially bored me and made me dizzy with the confusing noise of screaming crowds. Besides, as far as I could tell, the only two choices between these sports were to watch someone scratch his crotch and spit, or watch a bunch of guys hug each others buns and pour champagne on each other. To me, that was like getting a choice between being shot or stabbed.

Other things in the toy drawer sometimes included samples of perfume or lotion, small plastic scoops which may have come out of cake mix boxes or laundry detergent, a plastic squeaky fish and wooden salt and pepper shakers. Many of these items ended up coming home with me.

I remember the plastic scoops being sort of marquise-shaped with a handle at the end, and being molded in red or yellow plastic. I halfway remember them saying something like "Betty Crocker" or "Duncan Hines" on them, but I'm not sure if that's where they came from. It seemed that they were made in the different colors to distinguish two sizes from each other. There may have been some mixes that took more or less of some added ingredient. I'm not sure.

One of the times we were there, they happened to have a bunch of these scoops in the drawer. I took them out and was playing with them for a long time. I don't remember everything I was doing with them, but I ended up stacking a bunch of them on top of each other. I had some of the other toys out too. Later I think I was pretending to make a recipe of something as I measured air with each scoop. Near the end of the day, I realized that it would probably be too greedy of me to expect to be able to take all these things home. It seemed that I would have to leave some of the items there for next time. I didn't know how to bring up the subject that it would be good to have them all without seeming piggy, so I timidly asked my aunt, "what if I took them all?" I think she heard, "stacked" instead of "took". Her answer was, "They'd fall!" I was totally confused, and if I'd had a hard time asking the question the first time, I certainly wasn't going to repeat it. I didn't bring it up again, but I think I did end up being allowed to take a lot of stuff home that time.

About 6 years after we'd moved away from that area, we went back for a visit. That trip was detailed in my last book. I've often referred to it as "The St. Louis Disaster Trip". But one of the things we did manage to do on that trip amid the chaos that ensued, was to go to the zoo. That's when I discovered that the bear we all remembered from the toy drawer at Grandma's was sold in the gift shop there. My sister got one. In the days following, my brother, for some reason, decided the bear was his and kept taking it from my sister. We went back to the zoo and got another one for him so he'd stop tormenting her, and I got one this time, too. My sister showed hers to my aunt, and she commented that she still had hers from all those years ago. I remember hers being pretty worn; probably because we all played with it when we came. I don't know how long she had it before we got to it.

The toy drawer, however, was a great thing to look forward to each time. I've since collected a basket of toys for kids who come around to play at our house – whether they may be nieces, nephews, great-nieces or neighbors. They all know where to find them, and the youngest one, not yet two at the time, has already asked about them when she couldn't find them. Temporarily stashed in another room while the Christmas tree was up, the basket wasn't in its usual place, and she was puzzled by the lack of "box" in the corner. I knew exactly what she was looking for. And she got it from this pushover.

20. Grandma Meets Woody Woodpecker

In the mid-1960's, when I was about 5, my grandmother was in the hospital dying of colon cancer. I didn't know at the time, that her condition was that bad. When she died, I somehow got the idea, which I held onto for years, that she had had a heart attack. She did have a bad heart, but that wasn't what had ended her lifetime. I didn't find out until I was in my late 30's or early 40's, what had caused her demise.

One day, very close to the end of her life, we went to visit her in the hospital. The Christmas before, I had received a talking Woody Woodpecker puppet. I still remember the blue corduroy body, the white felt belly, the red and yellow plastic head with large white, black and blue eyes, and the red felt comb on its head.

We were sitting out in the visiting room, my entire family of 7, waiting for my grandma to come out from her room. I began pulling the puppet's string, causing the pre-recorded phrases to ring loudly. My mother stopped me with the usual explanatory phrases, "This is a hospital; we have to be quiet; people are trying to rest…" And so on.

Then my grandma came out. Seeing me with my puppet, she was thrilled, and began pulling its string.

"Hee hee hee HAAAA-Hooo!" the puppet screamed, echoing around the visiting room and through the halls of the hospital. My mother was mortified, and began to admonish her own mother.

"What's the big idea, Buster?" the puppet yelled, as my grandma, ignoring my mom's embarrassed and horrified countenance, continued pulling the string. "Timberrrrr! Time for lunch!"

Grandma was having the time of her life, and possibly for the LAST time in her life. Can't take Grandma anyplace nice – maybe that's why we were here. Maybe she was in her second or third childhood. In any case, she was cheered up at a gloomy time, and possibly created some laughs for surrounding patients, interrupting their somber moods for awhile. Or maybe she annoyed them. Hard to say which reaction she was hoping for – or got.

You never know... Grandma (and the other patients) may have gone to their rewards with one of this puppet's other phrases embedded firmly in their minds: "Hee hee hee HAAAA-Hooo! I love you! I do, I do, I do!!!"

21. They Lay Out Dead Horses, Don't They?

Shortly after I turned 5, I experienced the notion of death for the first time when both of my grandparents on my mom's side died within less than a month of each other. We had expected it with my grandma; she had been in the hospital as mentioned earlier, and was nearing the end. The odd thing was that my grandpa died first. We have all believed that he died of a broken heart. I remember hearing that he had begun brooding, and would sit in his chair all day and stare ahead, not wanting to eat or anything else. He died at home while my grandma was still struggling to hang on in the hospital. She followed him about 3 weeks later.

I had been confused about this for some time, because I remembered one phone call coming in the evening, and finding out again in the morning. I had thought they were both about my grandma. But when I questioned people about it years later, they figured out that the evening call was probably the one about my grandpa, and the news in the morning was the later information about my grandma. I only remember telling my brother about my grandma when they all came home from school later. I was in the afternoon kindergarten class, and would normally go back to school with my brothers and sister after they would come home for lunch. This time, however, my mom told everybody we were leaving immediately after lunch for St. Louis, and wouldn't be going back to school that day.

So we made 2 extra trips to St. Louis that year. We normally went there about 4 times a year for various holidays and part of the summer, but this time we were there for very short trips for the funerals and surrounding days to get things in order. Both of them had been born and had died in February. A short enough month it was, without having added complications.

I remember standing with my mom at my grandma's casket, and seeing her lying in there. I seem to remember her wearing light blue satin. Often, I have considered buying pale blue satin nightgowns, but have always been stopped by the idea that I would look dead. It's a personal thing; I doubt that anyone else would think that, unless they also remember this, are reading this or have been told about this incident. I don't even know if I'm right about what she was wearing; others who were questioned didn't remember. I do remember though, having my mom tell me I could touch Grandma if I wanted to; she seemed to be trying to allay any fears I may have had. I don't believe I was able to make myself do it though, at least not for long.

Shortly after this, I must have had a need to act out the deaths of others in my play-time activities. I remember having a red plastic tray that came out of a box of cookies. For some reason, the Girl Scout cookies called Thin Mints come to mind, but I don't know if those ever had a plastic tray in the box, or if they were always wrapped in the cellophane tubes like they have now. This was a flavor from way back that has held on all these years, though I think they used to be yellow inside instead of the chocolate mint cookie they have now, and they were dipped in the chocolate with added mint flavor. Still, they haven't retired this variety, even as they've added new ones over the years. It seems to be a classic favorite.

It does seem that the Hydrox cookies had a red plastic tray in them, but I thought it was one with 4 channels to stack the cookies in rather than the single one I remember. Maybe they did use those in Thin Mints back then.

Anyway, this one was empty and had been given to me to play with. I decided to turn it upside down and use it for a building. And what kind of building should it be, but a funeral parlor! It had to have been the freshest thing in my mind at the time.

It was too short to be for any of the dolls I had at that time. But I did have a collection of small plastic horses, including a very tiny white one. I decided this would be the deceased, and the others would be coming to visit.

For part of the time, I laid the horse on its side outside the building to make sure the other horses would know where to come. But once in awhile, I would move it inside where it belonged. It seemed that I alternated this for a long time, as I continued to have the other horses arrive. And I left it set up for awhile, until I was ordered to pick up my toys. You know, "They can do it!"

I don't know how many times I played that game, or if it helped work out my confusion over my grandparents' deaths. But, rather than being morbid, I thought it was a bit creative.

Do horses go to funerals? Maybe, in the military or in England. I think I saw them on TV for Ronald Reagan. But they're usually not paying their respects to their equine friends, as far as I know!

22. Who Started this Punny Business?

I specialize in bad puns. Always have, and probably always will. It's incurable. I've checked it out with the professionals. It may be in my genes, but as I've bought new jeans, it hasn't gotten better. I believe I am stuck with it for life.

The groans that come up as a result are the measure of how badly I've smacked someone's punny bone. Also, the length of time it takes to drive the point home to their realization.

I don't believe I was born with this condition, though. I believe it was cultivated by years of reading the Jokes and Riddles in that classic children's magazine known as Highlights.

I cannot remember a time in my young life when these magazines were not in our house. Being the youngest of five kids, I not only read the ones that came for me, but also the ones that were left over from the other four. We had quite a collection.

And the joke and riddle columns were not written by their editors. Kids could send in their favorites, and hope for publication. Normally they were not made up by the kids either, just the best they had heard somewhere. There were, however, a very select few that I've never heard anywhere else.

In any case, this magazine started me on my own career of making up as many as I could. It became a habit; without any attempts on my part, I would suddenly find myself coming up with a comeback for almost any statement. Maybe you could say that my humor was fully *groan* at an early age.

Many times, as a kid, I would remind my mom of something, only to have her answer, "I'm aware!" To this, I would quickly add, "wolf!" and duck out of her way. I was often referred to as a "brat".

Every group I have ever been in, I have either driven people nuts or fired them up with my puns. Most people have come to expect it from me, and manage to figure things out early on.

One of my favorite riddles from Highlights, which was in one of the issues in the mid '60s was this:

Q. What did the sick elevator say?

A. I'm coming down with something

Somehow I didn't notice that one until the magazine was a few months old. But it stuck, because it was one of the first times I had heard of being able to pun with a whole sentence instead of just one word.

Years later, I had surgery for an ingrown toenail and asked the podiatrist ahead of time if I could drive myself home. He said I could. I answered, "That's good, because otherwise I'd have to call a toe truck!" Then I mentioned it would be all right as long as someone else would foot my bill.

That last one came from a time a number of years earlier when I was participating in a craft boutique. Someone had suggested that besides selling our craft items, we should also include cookies and other such nasty items for sale to draw in all of the people who were ruled by their stomachs. I bought cookie cutters in the shape of a hand and a foot and made cookies with cinnamon candy toenails and fingernails. After wrapping them individually in plastic wrap, I piled them in a basket to set on my table, and added a sign that read, "Need a hand? Foot my bill!"

Recently someone asked, "What's a carbuncle?"

My answer: "It's what you use to fasten your seatbelt!"

My priest will often explain to people what a catechumen is. My explanation is a little different than his, as I often add, "If you open the door, the cat'll cum in!"

About 4-1/2 years ago, I received a handicapped placard from the DMV because I messed up my left knee in 1985. I've had surgery and been through a lot of exercise programs to strengthen it, but it still flares up often. I've had a number of times when people have called to me as I'm getting out of my car and asked if I have the placard. They seem to think I'd try to get away with using a close parking space I'm not qualified for. It must be because I look so young and spry. One guy even stood in front of my sister's car and craned his neck looking at the windshield until I put the placard up. And I don't think he was a security guard or a cop.

Therefore, I've gotten a great thrill out of people who park crooked in a space and don't bother to straighten out, abandoning their vehicles in a crazy cockeyed position. This gives me the opportunity to comment, to the irritation of my sister,

"NOW *THERE'S* A CASE OF HANDICAPPED PARKING!"

23. My Name's Red – I Live Near the Meat District

Going shopping with my parents as a kid was a major thrill. A chance to get out of the house, go for a ride, see what was out there and maybe mooch something good. I looked forward to it.

Depending on the store or shopping center, there were a lot of different things to look for each time. In one mall there was a sign painted on the wall in the underground parking lot that had an orange and white diagonal striped background. I always thought it looked like a giant piece of Fruit Stripe gum.

In another shopping center were various statues of pioneer life. There was a covered wagon pulled by oxen and led by the man of the household walking alongside. As you gazed at the ends of the wagon where the cover was tied, you could see his wife, child and dog looking out the "window" holes. In front of other stores in that center were statues of a cowboy wrestling a steer with its tongue hanging out, (not the cowboy's – the steer's), and an Indian on a horse chasing a buffalo, spear held high. The garbage cans throughout the center were mostly made to look like tree stumps, although one was a shock of wheat. Leaning against, or perched on top of each stump was an animal – a skunk, raccoon, fawn, etc. The shock of wheat had a large skunk sitting next to it holding its nose. I have pictures of most of these, taken when I went back there in 1981.

The Indian's white horse had a strange black mark on its butt, which I had always thought was a brand, or a spot of color on the horse, like a palomino or appaloosa might have. There was a big spot in the middle with longer ones coming out of it, like flower petals. Only when I took a picture years later, did I figure out what it might possibly have been. Perhaps some kid had tried to pet the buffalo when the black paint on the ruff around its neck was still wet. Then, needing to get the paint off his hands, he may have smacked the horse's butt, leaving a small handprint. I didn't think of this until I was home and had my pictures developed, therefore I wasn't able to go check the statue for details in the paint.

I was especially fond of one grocery store that had a lobster tank, complete with live lobsters roaming around in it. I would sometimes ask to go see it if we hadn't been in that area of the store yet. How quaint and considerate, I thought, that the management would put in an aquarium for customers to enjoy as they shopped! I had no way of knowing at the time, what it was really for!

How could I have known that these guys were waiting in line for the Butter Bath, Soup Spa or Steam Room? It was a bit unnerving, years later when I finally discovered what that was all about.

...Reminds me of one of my brothers. A number of years ago, when he had live chickens, he let them roam loose on his property. The only rule he had was that they weren't allowed on the porch or inside the house. Whenever he'd spot one on his porch, he'd run after it, yelling, "Soup Pot!" and scare it off. Over the years, he lost them all to freezing weather, dogs, possible heart attacks from screaming at them, etc.

I still eat lobster when I can get it. I just don't buy them while I can look them in the eye and have them look back.

24. We Don't Smile in my Profession

We had, in our parish in Kansas, an Irish priest who was the pastor. I remember him being a big rock - a wall of a man, not unlike Mt. Rushmore in both stiffness and stature; only the faces were different. He always struck me as being a lump, an unmoving object. I don't remember ever hearing him preach – just seeing him around and seeing pictures of him in the school yearbook. They only made one of those, the year I was in kindergarten, and I still have parts of it. The plastic spiral that bound the book fell apart years ago from my overuse of looking for people I knew. I kept as many pages as I could, some getting lost or misplaced in the transit of moving several times. There were at least two pictures of this priest in the yearbook. Both of them showed him looking somewhat grumpy, with a hard, straight line for a mouth.

One year on his anniversary, someone decided to hold a party in his honor. I don't remember if it was a surprise party or not. I just remember a lot of food, (I think it was a potluck), and a couple tons of people crowding the parish hall.

This may or may not have been the time that we were all heading out the door when the event was over, and I turned to my mom and asked, "what if you were as fat as the door?" I was famous for "what if" questions at the time, and drove my mom crazy with them. This time, she turned to one of our neighbors, who was also my aunt's aunt, (I didn't know that for years), and repeated my question to her. They both laughed as we went out.

Sometime during this event, I heard my mom remark to someone that this priest's face was going to hurt the next day from smiling so much. I looked up and saw him greeting a throng of people, grinning broadly as he met with each one. I somehow took this comment of my mom's to mean that priests didn't normally smile, or weren't supposed to. I chewed on it for awhile, wondering why this was.

And then, sometime in the next few days, I was playing on the living room floor and just had to know the answer to this. I asked my mom, "Why aren't priests supposed to smile?"

She had no idea what I was talking about. I suspect that she hadn't meant for me to hear her verbal observation, spoken in light sarcasm. I clarified my question by saying, "well… you said this guy's face was going to hurt the next day!"

She remembered now, and explained to me that she meant that only for this priest, because she had rarely seen him smile. She may have also been careful about what she said around me after that.

25. Do Teeth Give Your Brown Bat Gas?

Who likes needles? Who likes watching someone yank a part of themselves out? Nobody that I know of. Until I was five, pulling teeth was just something that I had heard of happening to someone else. Then, I was told I had a small mouth. Tell that to my brothers!

Sometime into my sixth year, I was told I would have to have five teeth removed all at once. Something about making room in my mouth for my later teeth. I think the dentist decided on his own that it would be better for me to be put out with gas rather than being awake at that age for that long. I don't believe it was because I raised a fit. I think he was just being considerate because people usually don't get five out at one time.

I was taken to a clinic somewhere outside of where the dentist had his office. I don't remember how far it was from home, or even if it was within Kansas or over in Missouri. I never watched what road I was on if I wasn't driving, and I certainly wasn't driving at age 5! I was told I would be given gas to fall asleep and wouldn't feel a thing. I'm not sure I was told about the vile and horrendous smell.

After being led into my room and laid flat, someone came in and put the mask on my face. I had never smelled anything that bad. I don't know how much of the stench came from the gas and how much was from the rubber in the mask. I thought I was suffocating. I fought the mask until I finally succumbed to the stuff and went out like a light.

Soon I found myself on a tight pristine hospital bed with perfect sheet corners, frantically being pushed down a hallway by a bunch of nurses in their white uniforms. Every few seconds they would look back up the hallway in sheer fright. For there in the hospital hallway was a giant brown bat with a wingspan that spread almost all the way across the width of the hall. About four feet altogether of big, light brown wings were flapping as the thing chased us. How long this went on, I don't know, but I woke up tasting blood and being swollen with cotton like a hamster fills his pouches with seeds. I must have swallowed a lot of blood; I found myself getting sick several times that day, and re-tasting the stuff. The bat was still very clear in my mind, as were the looks of fear on the nurses' faces as they periodically checked the distance between us and the big animal.

Before I went home that day, someone gave me a small plastic box with all 5 of my teeth in it. I still have it somewhere. It is pink on the bottom with a clear top and the words "My Tooth" printed on the clear part. The nurse explained that in this case, it should say, "My Teeth", but they didn't have one like that.

A few years later after we had moved to California, I had a nasty toothache. I was either 7 or 8. I had already gotten to know the dentist we had chosen, and I got major heebie-jeebies from him. He was a very jumpy sort of guy – kind of hyperactive, got down to business right away, and I always felt like a machine he was working on. I only needed to walk into his waiting room and smell the familiar medicinal scent of the place to get nervous. When he told me he was going to have to pull this tooth, I wasn't about to let him. I kept screaming, "Oh no!" when he'd try to stick the needle in my mouth, and he kept answering, "Oh yes!" Finally when he was afraid he would stick himself, rendering his hand numb and useless for the rest of the day, he had his receptionist make an appointment at another of these places that would put me out. I was allowed to get out of his chair and go out to the waiting room, thinking I had won. I walked out there in time to hear the receptionist tell my mom, "Tomorrow morning at nine o'clock." (It might have been 8:00). She was given the address of some place near O'Connor Hospital in San Jose. It was right before Christmas, I believe, and at that time there was a giant Santa Claus that sat on top of the Macy's store right near there. Maybe that was supposed to comfort me. But how did I know if the bat had followed me to California, and how could I take that smell again?

The afternoon before, I tried to comfort myself by pretending that one of my dolls had a birthday the next day. It was Midge, who was either a friend or cousin of Barbie. She had red hair and freckles, at least mine did. I think you could get all of those Barbie friends and relatives in various hair colors, and later, different races. Mine had a teacher's outfit that I think I got separately after I'd been given the doll. It was a red dress that was mostly solid colored on top and checked on the bottom. It came with a small book to put in her hand and a plastic globe that turned on an axis. I started chanting something about her birthday being tomorrow, so I could temporarily forget that I was about to be butchered.

By the time I got to the clinic the next day, I was close to hysterical, picturing what it was going to be like. This was only one tooth instead of five, but it was still the act of undergoing the gas mask that freaked me out. One of the nurses chided me, saying there was a girl in the next room about my age who was having the same thing, and she was totally calm. It was insinuated, and maybe even verbalized that I was being a baby, and this other girl was taking it perfectly calmly. Good for her. Maybe she'd never had it done before, or maybe she hadn't had the experiences I'd had with doctors in the past. I wanted to punch that nurse.

They finally did come in with the mask and stuck it over my nose. I put up another fight like last time, until I was subdued.

And was the bat there? You bet he was! In the same manner as last time, he flapped down the hallway, slowly and casually. There was one difference, though. The bed, the nurses, me – everything else was gone! We were nowhere to be seen. Had we turned the corner or had that thing eaten us all in one bite, including the bed? I never did find out, as I woke up once again, sick, swollen and tasting nasty.

Maybe all of this was the reason why, when I had another nasty toothache a year or two later, around the same time of year, I let my regular dentist pull it. It was the first time I was awake for this, and I think I surprised the dentist by saying he could do it. But I still didn't like being in his office. Except for the treasure chest where I could pick a prize at the end, and the receptionist named Val, who always greeted me nicely and talked to me, there was nothing good about being in there. Years later, when I was about 16 or 17, my mom finally found out that his office had always scared me from the second I walked in and smelled it. I changed dentists, and have had several since, as I've found myself with different insurance every few years. I'm still not crazy about going to anyone, but at least nobody else has had whatever caused that smell. I can still remember it if I think hard enough.

In any case, the brown bat is gone. Sometimes I consider having somebody put me out again so I can see if it would still happen. I don't think they use the same stuff they used to use. I have had something intravenously when I've had other surgeries, but it doesn't have the same effect. Maybe the bat has had enough to eat. After all these years, it's probably dead anyway.

If they still do use the gas method somewhere, it's probably better that I don't request it, now that I think about it. Consider what the next dream would be in the series. I'd probably wind up in a pile of bat guano in the hospital hallway with the *bat* nowhere to be seen!

26. I Hate Socks

All three of my brothers were Boy Scouts. My sister was a Girl Scout. Both of my parents were in the leadership of the Scouting program. I was the only one who defected by going off into Camp Fire Girls in later years.

Because of my parents' leadership in Scouting, we were often forced to go to meetings for our siblings, such as awards dinners in the parish hall of our church, etc. One thing I hated the most was being required to go to "Girl Scout Day Camp" (said with a sneer) in the summertime. It was only a few hours each day, but the groups were divided by age, so I never knew anyone in the group I was stuck in. Nor did I know any of the counselors I had to listen to and obey. They didn't know me either, and had to get used to the fact that I didn't talk to adults. They probably had that fact explained to them ahead of time. But I was so bored, and I never did get into playing group games like "Red Rover". I would just sit and watch them, and wish the day would end. One year we had two kids named Susan in our group, so someone decided at the beginning of summer that the older one would be called, "Susan" and the younger "Susie". They wanted to avoid confusion from the start, and both Susans agreed.

Around 1965 or 1966, possibly in the year before we moved from Kansas to California, our entire family went to Philmont Scout Ranch in New Mexico. I'm not sure if that was just a big thing to do before we moved or if there was a chance for my parents to get more training for running the Scout meetings. In any case, the whole family went.

During the days, we were again separated into different areas for our various age groups. I remember a few people from my group, but not many names. It seemed that there were two girls named Marcia, and all I could think of when I heard their names was Marshmallow. I had never heard the name before. There was also a younger girl, maybe my age or a little younger, who didn't speak clearly. When one of the counselors was teaching us a new song, she announced that she knew that one, and sang along. Only, her version was, "Da more we get to-ged-der, da happier we'll be!" That stuck in my mind.

I remember two counselors – an older lady named Marge and a younger one, possibly a teenager, named Tina. One day Tina told some of us that her real name was Christine. I had never heard of Tina being a nickname; I figured it was just another name. I had never known anyone with that name in those days, and it always reminded me either of Tiny or Tuna. One day, someone asked her, "Tina, what's your nickname?" She answered, "Tina", and retold what I had already heard – that her full name was Christine.

Marge would often come out on the playground with us and push us on the swings. They had new equipment in a shiny red enameled metal, and the first time we went out, she advised us, "our metal cuts!" She wanted to let us know not to touch the edges.

My parents bought me a turquoise ring, the design being something like a flower with one small round stone in the center and about six of them around the outside in a circle. One day, after playing in the sandbox in front of the room our family was staying in, I couldn't find my ring. I thought it had fallen off in the sand. I went back out to dig and see if I could find it. An older kid had a spoon, and he thought he could help me find it faster if he used that to dig. The only problem there was that he dug quickly and flipped the sand behind him. It wasn't long before a bunch flicked into my eyes.

A German lady who was nearby took me back to my room since I couldn't see, and someone helped me rinse out my eyes. I think the kid who flipped the sand was pretty upset, but I believe he was reassured that it wasn't his fault;

he was only trying to help. To make things worse, I think we ended up finding the ring in our room later. Either that, or my dad went out to the sandbox later and found it. I'm not sure which.

And then there were the naps. During the daytime hours that we had to be with our groups, the little kids had to take naps on the floor. That might have been all right, except there was one requirement that made me rebel heavily. They made us take off our shoes.

And I would cry. Not just a little, and not quietly, as I normally might have. We're talking about screaming bloody murder. Because I didn't talk to anyone, the counselors couldn't figure out what my problem was. And why did this happen every day?

They talked to my mom about it at some point, and she decided I must be missing my doll. I had her in bed with me every night; I had brought her on the trip for night use, but I didn't take her with me to the day classes. My mom arranged to put her in a bag every day and send her with me to be stashed on a shelf until nap time. They thought it was worth a try.

But it didn't work. If they had only known the full reason for this, they may have made an exception about making me take my shoes off. For, I had always hated socks. Especially dirty ones and ones with holes in them. They made me sick. And it was worse when I'd have them on under shoes for awhile and have to take the shoes off, revealing wetness that would get cold and slimy real fast. It drove me stark-raving nuts, and still does. When I would go to a shoe store and have to take my old shoes off to try on new ones, I was constantly urged to "uncurl the toes". It was too gross; if I could keep them tucked under, they didn't get as much air and didn't seem so wet. But they had to be uncurled to measure my foot and to check the length inside the shoe. The latter wasn't such a problem – by the time my feet were back in shoes, the problem wasn't as bad. But I couldn't stand that bit of cloth that would sometimes hang off my toe if I didn't get it on all the way.

Years later, I worked with a guy who acted like he was one of my brothers. As if three weren't enough! At one time, Chuck worked right behind me. He used to take the rubber feet that we put on the bottom of the computers we were building and throw them at me, bouncing them off my head and back. When I'd turn around, he'd feign innocence.

This guy found out early on that I hated socks. He also learned that dirt and holes made them more disgusting to me. He started talking to me about dirty socks with various kinds of food in them. His favorite was, "dirty socks with hot mayonnaise". He said this to me all the time. And he claimed the holes were for putting straws through for sucking out the hot mayonnaise. Gross, he was.

Chuck rode the bus to work, and on the way to work from the bus stop one day, he found an old sock in the street. It was too good to pass up. He picked it up, and farther down the road, found a greasy paper bag to put it in. He brought it in and left it on my workbench. When I opened the bag, I immediately knew who it was from.

There was a way to get back at him. Chuck was a vegetarian who got sick at the sight of meat. I knew exactly what to do. I went to the pet section at the grocery store and bought a dog toy – a nice big rubber turkey leg.

I flashed this at him a number of times during the day. It did the trick – until finally he said, "Don't show me your legs!"

I also remember the time he wore a very old holey sock to work. It was just about falling apart. Several times during that day, he called my name and I looked back. He had taken off his shoe, and was showing me the entire bottom of his foot through numerous holes. He told me later he had planned on throwing it away, but thought he should get the most fun out of it with me first. How kind! How I wish he could have been in my group at Philmont when we had to take naps. He could have listened to me scream wildly without knowing what caused it, and been driven nuts.

There were good things at Philmont. I thought the playground was fun and there was one night when we ate buffalo sloppy-joes. Near the end, when some of the older kids were getting awards for their Scouting deeds, the counselors made sure that each of the younger groups got something just for being there. Everybody in my group got a small plaster plaque that was shaped like the head of a white donkey. The tongue had been painted pink, and some of the features had been outlined in black. I think it said, "Philmont" on a straight section at the bottom of the neck.

A few years ago, I had a podiatrist tell me I should have closed toed shoes with socks to prevent sores that could become a later danger to a diabetic. I told him socks had made me throw up since I was a kid. His answer was, "you sound like my three-year-old daughter!"

Well, yeah, that may have been when it started, but I think it was earlier!

27. Pinecone Energy

What kid doesn't want the fastest tricycle, bicycle, wagon or other kid vehicle in town? The problem is that they don't make tricycles with multiple speeds like they do with bicycles; at least they didn't when I was a kid. I don't know if they've gotten fancier now, but I don't think so. The speed depends on how fast the kid can pedal.

That didn't stop me from trying to develop a power capsule, though. The people across the street from us had a pine tree – a big old thing that spread and bore many cones, dropping them on the lawn and in the street. I never saw one that was open – just the slender, closed, elongated egg-shaped ones. They may have been a different variety; maybe they never did open.

One day I was out riding my tricycle, a dark blue model with an orange seat which I believe had been in the family awhile. There was also a larger red one, but I always found that too imposing. I don't think I ever switched to that one. I liked the little one, and used it until I got my first bicycle.

I was trying to pedal fast, but I was dissatisfied with my performance. Maybe I could devise something that would give my tricycle more energy. I found a few of these tightly closed pinecones and shoved them one by one under the metal seat, wedging them in firmly so they'd stay. I think I managed to fit six or seven in there. Each time I'd put another in there, I'd try pedaling again, and it seemed to add some power with each one. At least in my head and my legs.

I had been at this for awhile when, stopping to rest on the sidewalk, I noticed another pinecone in the gutter. Somehow it didn't cross my mind that this was a different one than the ones I had shoved under the seat. Instead, I was sure I had lost it, and needed to retrieve it.

I don't think anyone had ever warned me that you needed to get off a tricycle before bending over, especially if you were up on a curb and were reaching toward the lower gutter. I bent over, thinking I could reach the pinecone and pick it up without much effort. But before I knew it, I was facedown in the graveled street. I think I was across the street in front of a neighbor's house at the time. I'm pretty sure that's where the tree was, and I think I had gone over there to find the most pinecones for my power capsules. I seem to remember the lady who sold the World Book Encyclopedias being on her route in the neighborhood and seeing me. I'm not sure, but I think she may have been the one to take me home, having recognized me. Either that, or the guy across the street brought me home and the lady was already in our living room. I do halfway remember this neighbor bringing my tricycle home later, which had been left near his home. That may have been a different time, though, because I also have memories of being right in front of our house when I fell, rather than across the street.

By the time I was cleaned up, it was possible to pinpoint and count the numerous sores on my face. I'm not sure I ever knew the number myself, but it was a lot. They stood out later when they all turned to scabs, prompting questions from my first grade classmates and teacher. One boy, Mark, gave me a somber recital of what could happen if a rock got underneath my biggest scab. What were the chances of that happening? Maybe a piece of gravel from the street, but I don't think even that would be small enough. Sand would be more likely, but I still didn't think he should have gone into so much detail to scare me. He probably thought he was helping by warning me.

One day, shortly after this accident, our teacher wanted us each to write a story about ourselves. I didn't know what to write except my name, age and similar details. My teacher suggested that I tell how my accident happened. Not being into writing much yet, I didn't think to go into detail about the mishap. So after my vital statistics, I ended my story with the line, "I fell on my face in the street".

I showed it to my parents when I brought it home, and my dad felt the need to read it out loud. I always hated that. Don't spread my stuff to the whole world! When he got to the last line, both of my parents laughed. I do believe I told them to shut up, complete with a frown. They got upset at that, but I don't think I got in trouble. Maybe they figured out it wasn't supposed to be a joke. They may have explained that they were only laughing at the surprise sentence at the end of my name and age, etc. But I think I might have trained them, at least partway, at that time. At least that was one of their first lessons in not laughing at kids' wording of things.

My face healed and besides that, I was riding my tricycle again. I don't think I ever stopped, except for the brief time I recuperated the first day. I do remember looking under the seat sometime after that, counting and noticing that I hadn't lost any pinecones in the accident. The one in the street had been just a stray; maybe even a bomb thrown from the tree to tell me to stop picking up its cones.

28. The Story Behind "Dickie's in the Back Seat Barfin'"

Those who read my first book, "Sublime to Ridiculous" may remember seeing the lyrics to this song. However, some may be wondering how it came about.

Depending on whether you know me or not, you may or may not be surprised that it is a semi-true story. Here's a refresher on the words, before I launch into my brother's time of misery and my opus 8 years later:

> *I remember one day*
> *My mom came to pick me up from school*
> *My brother was lyin' on the seat of the car*
> *He got hit in the head, the old fool.*
> *Refrain: Dickie's in the back seat barfin'*
> *Dickie's in the back seat barfin'*
> *He thinks he's gonna die*
> *But he doesn't know why*
> *Dickie's in the back seat barfin'*
> *I walked over to the car*
> *On that cloudy day*
> *I tried to get in the back seat*
> *But I soon found barf at my feet. I said...(Refrain)*
> *When we got home that day*
> *We got out of the car*
> *But Dickie stayed, barfin' his life away*
> *I wouldn't be surprised if he'd been to a bar. (Refrain)*
> *Well, Dickie stayed through the end of the day*
> *And the back seat he did fill*
> *He stayed in there 'til the middle of May*
> *And for all I know he's barfin' still. (Refrain)*

It was 1965 or '66, my first grade year, and my brother's sophomore year in high school. I had been sent to another school in a different city because I had gone through my kindergarten year at the local Catholic school without saying a word to my teacher. This other school had a special education class, which they placed me in to start with, but I later moved to the regular first grade class. My brother had won a scholarship at a high school a few cities over from us. We both had to be driven to school, a new experience, since the Catholic school was right at the end of our street and we had usually walked.

My mother had gotten into a car pool with about 4 other mothers with boys going to the same high school. We had a Corvair then, and there were no laws about seat belts at the time, so I would often get up in the back window when all of these teenagers were cramming into this car. There was a space back there that I fit into perfectly. But we didn't always have all of them to take. I'm not sure if each of the drivers had a full week or just a day at a time. And we may not have gone to school at the same time. It's possible that the times I got into the back window were during my brother's freshman year, when I was only in kindergarten for half a day.

One rainy day in first grade, I came out of school and headed for the back seat of the car, which was waiting right out front. I was immediately directed to the front seat, with the revelation that my brother was stretched out in back.

Seems that he and a bunch of his bright friends from school had decided that a "fun" rainy day activity would be to go out and play touch football, sliding around in the mud. As a result, I believe my brother was elbowed in the head. My mother received a call from the school saying that he'd been hit in the head, was throwing up and needed to be picked up early.

Because of the time of day that this happened, there wasn't time to retrieve him, get him home and settled and get back over in that direction to pick me up at my school. Therefore, my mom had to make a quick swing to the elementary school with my brother still in the back seat. I believe there were a number of stops on the way, allowing my brother to stick his head out and relieve himself.

Whether we went right home so he could get to bed, or straight to the doctor's office, I don't remember, but we did find out at some point that he had a concussion.

Eight years later, I was at a park with my sister, and somehow managed to bring up the incident. My brother never went by "Dickie", even when he was little, but I often called him that. When I got to the part of the story where I was heading for the back seat of the car, I told my sister, "I was motioned to the front because Dickie was in the back seat."

And my sister answered, "Barfin'".

I immediately thought that sounded like a song title. "Dickie's in the Back Seat Barfin'". Could be a big hit, maybe even hit the top 10. At that time, one of the students at my school had written a poem describing what it was like to walk near the ocean and smell dead fish and mussels. One of the teachers was in the process of setting it to music. I decided to give him another project.

So, within the next few days, I wrote 3 verses and a refrain. I took it to school, and pretty soon I had a tape with my lyrics set to music.

Like I said, it was only a semi-true story. First of all, I didn't normally refer to him as an "old fool" – I just needed something that rhymed with "school". Originally I had the phrase "sunny day" in the second verse, but my brother informed me it was raining, resulting in a quicker onset of the event. And, since I hadn't opened the back door yet, I didn't get "barf at my feet". There was no suspicion that he'd been to a bar either – again that was a rhyming convenience.

Also, as mentioned, the fourth verse did not exist in the beginning. After some of the people at my school heard the song, one of the students suggested that it should be wrapped up with a verse ending with, "for all I know he's barfin' still". She thought it was still a little open at the end and needed closure.

I didn't add the last verse right away, but a few years later, I thought of one. And most of that verse had nothing to do with the truth.

He didn't stay in the car 'til the end of the day. He was put straight to bed when we got home, and rested for a long time. And he didn't fill up the back seat. I think he was able to feel it coming on, and asked to stop the car each time. He certainly didn't stay until May – I'm not even sure what month it was when it happened. And if he had been barfin' still, I don't think he'd still be living 41 years later.

So even though I wasn't driving in first grade, or as a teenager, I still had a poetic license.

29. I'm on a Different Plane

In 1966, the telephone company transferred my dad out to San Francisco, CA. The announcement, made at the dinner table set the whole family buzzing. I wasn't sure I was quite so thrilled as the rest of them about moving away from everybody I knew.

A day or so after we got the news, I was across the street at Greg and Kathy's house telling Kathy we were moving. I may have mentioned before that they traveled a lot in their jobs. I had heard them talk about San Francisco and Sausalito, so I knew they had heard of the area. When Kathy asked me where we were going, I couldn't exactly remember how to say it. Then I spotted a box of crackers on the kitchen counter. I pointed to the corner where it said, "Nabisco" and told her, "It sounds like that." She knew right away. One of her favorite phrases was, "are you serious?" and she said that to me right away. I always thought that sounded too formal for talking to a little kid. Didn't she know I was six years old? It seemed funny that she'd say that to me all the time.

Everything in our home was packed into boxes from the moving company a few days early and blue stickers with numbers on them were affixed to the boxes. We all went around looking at the different numbers, wondering what they meant to the movers. Some of my brothers were excited to discover that one box said 007 on it. Maybe that's the one that had the guns in it. I don't think so. As far as I know, we only had toy guns that were my brothers' and a BB gun that was my dad's.

We'd had a wooden sandbox in our back yard that my dad had built years ago. It had gotten old, and the wood was crawling with worms. A couple of years before we moved, the family next door was getting ready to move, and didn't want to take their sandbox with them. Theirs was not a wooden box, but an old truck tire they'd gotten, maybe from a gas station, and set on its side in their back yard, filling it about halfway with sand. They agreed to give this to us, though we'd have to get our own sand, since the tire didn't have a bottom to keep their sand in when it was moved from one yard to another. Also, the sand had to be replaced every so often because neighborhood cats would often assume it was a community toilet. They never left me a dime though. I just knew that when I dug too deep and the mud underneath started smelling bad, it was a sign to clean and change it.

When we were getting ready to move, I thought we would be bringing this tire with us. Instead, my mom suggested giving it to the family who now lived in the house where it had originally been. They had kids now, and one was old enough to play in it. I didn't want to give it up, but my mom was trying to come up with a reason not to cart it to California. "It really is Maura's sandbox," she said in front of Maura and her mom. I gave in reluctantly. Later, after we had moved, we got a letter from these people which contained the sentence, "It really wasn't that big a deal about the tire, Loretta." By then, we were settled into our new house with a lot of new surroundings and we didn't know what the lady was talking about. It was only a number of years later that the sentence came back to me, and it suddenly dawned on me that she was saying I hadn't needed to give up my sandbox if I didn't want to. I was too old for it by the time the meaning of her letter sank into my mind.

One day, after we had watched our cars and a bunch of these boxes being loaded on moving vans in front of our old Kansas home, we waited for a taxi that had been called to our home. We would not be going to the airport right away, but would be staying in a motel for a night and leaving the next morning.

The people next door, the ones who had gotten our sandbox, stood on the sidewalk to see us off. At that time, their older girl was about 1-1/2 and their younger one, about six months. Another baby was born to that family about a year or so after we moved, and we found this out when we received a photograph at Christmas time with a third kid in it, a three-month-old girl. My sister was somewhat indignant that they hadn't told us another baby was coming.

As the parents of this family waved us off, the six-month-old baby screamed her head off until she was bright red. I'm sure it wasn't because we were moving; she was a bit young to notice that. I was pretty sure she was either wet or hungry, and I thought at the time that her parents shouldn't be ignoring her as they concentrated on us taking off. I thought they should take care of that girl before she blew a head gasket.

All seven of us piled into this taxi, which was being driven by a somewhat weathered, but smiling, older man. My dad told him we wanted to go to the Prom. I had no idea what the Prom was; it turned out it was a motel, possibly near the airport so we could get started first thing in the morning.

"Prom?" the driver said with a slight accent on the 'o', which many years later I came to associate with Michigan, or maybe Wisconsin. He smiled at all of us as we crammed into his cab, and promptly took off. It wasn't long before we checked into our room.

I remember little about the motel stay - only that there was a small red rectangular button near the curtains in our room that said, "Push". I'm not sure if it was for turning on a light or opening the curtains. I don't think there would have been an electronic setting for opening the curtains, especially in 1966. It may have been attached to the cords on the curtains rather than on the wall as I thought I remembered.

In any case, I believe we only stayed one night, and made our way to the airport the next morning.

I don't remember anything about that morning, before getting on the plane. I only remember that later on in the day, I was pretty sure I wouldn't live to see California.

We got our seats and waited for takeoff. Sometime later, a stewardess came by with a very large bowl of assorted candy and shoved it under my face, in my lap. All for me? My mom let me know that I could pick one thing. Geez! How chintzy! Sticking that giant bowl in front of me and then busting my bubble like that! I think my mom suggested the stick of gum, since it would help pop my ears if needed later.

And it definitely was needed later. For this, the first flight for most of my family members was fraught with turbulence. It was, one of the most freaky things I'd had to deal with at that stage of my life.

Sometime into the flight, the captain told us we could remove our seat belts. Most of us did, and we got up to move around a bit. It seemed to me, though, that every time I would take a step, the plane would lurch.

"I'm gonna die!" I screamed several times. Heads turned from all the way up the cabin.

My mom tried to keep me calm, but it was getting worse. More lurching, perfectly timed with my steps.

"I'm gonna die!" I thought it would never end. We were all in for a long flight, in more ways than one.

The strange thing, which most people didn't realize, was that I was sure it was my walking around that was making the plane wobble and jump. Me, a not yet seven-year-old peanut weighing very little - could I possibly be causing this large craft to do the hustle in the sky? Not likely, but it was too in-sync to be anything else, I thought.

I may have spent most of the flight in my seat with the seat belt on to prevent even more of this panic-induced screaming. Possibly, this was suggested by my mom in an effort to keep the other passengers sane. I'm not sure, but it did seem to last a long slow time. Kansas to California – how long does that take?

Once we got into the San Francisco Airport, I remember sitting around in one area while my dad got our luggage. We may have also been staying somewhere for the first night, so we might have had to get a shuttle or cab; I don't remember. I just know that a lady who was either a stewardess, or worked in the airport came over to talk to the rest of our family, welcoming us to California.

She approached my brother, two years older than I. Their conversation went something like this.

"What's your name?"

"Jon"

"Where are you from, Jon?"

My brother looked slightly confused. He turned to my mom, giggling a bit.

"Where am I from?" (Don't tell me this lady doesn't know!)

"Kansas!" my mom said, laughing as if he were from Mars.

I don't think the airport lady went much further than that. I don't remember if she talked to any of the others. Certainly not to me, since I didn't talk to many adults at the time. If she did, she didn't get an answer from me, and therefore went on.

We finally got to wherever we were to stay for the night; I know it wasn't our new house. We would find out about that later.

30. Monster Hands

We got a surprise when we moved to California. Our house wasn't finished being built. The builders had underestimated the amount of time it would take to get things finished. As it turned out, some of our future neighbors decided to rent an apartment in another city, and others stayed in a motel close to where our houses would be.

The first thing I remember was that our family was waiting in an office somewhere, and another family was there at the same time. I'm not sure if it was the office at the motel. I think it was the real estate office, and we were all being told that our houses weren't ready.

This other family had a girl who looked my age. Turned out, she was 23 days younger. This meant something to me at the time; I hardly ever met anyone who was younger. She came over to me and asked, "Are you going to live in Old Orchard?" I noticed a scrape on her upper lip, in a place where I couldn't imagine anyone bumping into anything. I had no idea what she meant by "Old Orchard", and I shrugged at her. I found out later that this was the area of Sunnyvale we were moving into. Cherry and apricot orchards were being thinned out and the lots readied for building houses, with a few trees left here and there for people to enjoy in their yards. This girl became my neighbor and my good friend for two years until her family moved again.

Years later, when my brother was managing the restaurant in Yosemite, this ex-neighbor came in to apply for a summer job. My brother was sitting across from her, reading her name over and over to himself as he tried to remember where he'd heard it. When he finally figured it out, he didn't let on that he knew who she was. He just looked up at her and said, "Oh, did you used to live at (quoted address)?" It had been about 9 years since she'd moved away, and she got a weird look on her face. She looked at him and said, "What kind of checking up do they *do* around this place?" He hired her.

Once we had checked into this motel where we had to stay for our first few weeks in California, we spent a lot of time with the various recreational activities available there. My brothers played a lot of shuffleboard, something I'd never seen before. It was hot, and we all spent a lot of time in the swimming pool. Sitting around in the pool each day, I began to notice certain people who seemed to have been staying there as long as we had. I was told they would be our neighbors. At the time, I didn't know our houses weren't finished. A girl in a one-piece black swimming suit was to be our neighbor two houses in one direction. A tall boy who turned out to be my brother's age would be two houses in the other direction from us.

It seemed we went out to breakfast every morning, usually to a place called, "Uncle John's Pancake House" and sometimes to Spivey's. I don't even remember where the first place was, and it's not there anymore. We did get to know it well, though, and it was the first time I had ever heard of boysenberries. One of the flavors of syrup they had available was boysenberry, and some of my brothers delighted in calling it, "poison berry". We thought it was fun to imagine we were pouring poison on our food and eating it all. I believe I only tried it once, going back to maple after that, as I was used to it.

I got a major surprise myself, the first day we were in our room. I stepped outside to look around and see how far I might venture out on my own, which was something I had always been afraid to do. I was always afraid of getting lost, no matter where I went. This time I thought I'd be braver. It didn't last, as I looked down the outdoor corridor, and saw something that made me go back quickly.

Two very large, dark green hands were reaching around the corner at the end of our building and waving up and down as if to grab the next kid who would come by. I ran back to our room.

After I explained to my family what I had seen, one of my brothers came out with me to investigate. That's when I probably got laughed at by everyone. Having never seen a philodendron, especially one this big with its long fingers on each leaf, I set myself up for a lot of teasing. One thing, though - once I was told it was a plant, I was able to go up to it often and dare it to get me. There was no fear, once I got close to that leafy vegetation. The plant itself was large, and planted in the garden area around the side of the building, and before the next building, if there was one. Only two of the giant "hands" were visible from the other end, where our room was.

The motel was nice enough for awhile, the plants were friendly once I got to know them, the pool was kind in hot weather and going out to breakfast every day was a delight. Still, it was good to get into our new house and get settled. There was still a lot of orchard left, a few jackrabbits still hopped through the semi-wild area, and there were a lot of clear lots where they hadn't gotten the houses built yet. Exploring was a daylong event in the area, as we found new things to check out every day for a long time.

31. The Quest For the Perfect Concrete Turtle

Even when our house and a few around us were done and occupied, there were still a lot of others that weren't. Big open lots made nice places to play in until frames of new houses started appearing in them. Often, my brothers and I would walk around in these lots after the construction workers had left, and pick up various things we'd find. There were a lot of round metal slugs that had been popped out of outlet boxes, and we'd pick them up to use for play money. We'd collect nails and small pieces of scrap lumber for building things at home. I thought I had found the greatest treasure when, one day I found a whole brick and brought it home.

I also noticed a lot of wet cement. Usually it would be a small pool that had either been spilled during the workday or poured off at the end of the day. Since it was still wet and soft, I thought it would make a perfect free substitute for modeling clay.

Almost every day, for a long time, I would scrape up a small handful of this stuff to take home. I would also find a small board to use as a working surface for the artistic creation I had in mind. It was, more often than not, and maybe even always, a turtle, that I planned to sculpt.

It was an easy enough thing to mold. All I needed to do was make a mound for the back, pinch out 4 legs from the sides and a tail in the back, and mold a head at the other end. After creating this masterpiece daily, I'd put the board in a safe place in the garage for it to dry, planning to come back the next day to check on it.

And each morning, my turtle would be cracked to bits! I couldn't understand it. I had purposely put it between the studs in the garage wall so it would be out of the way and couldn't be bumped. But it still would be shattered each time.

It was a long time before I gave up on this. Having never heard of catalysts at this time in my life, and having no idea how they got this stuff to harden evenly and properly, I was baffled, but kept trying each time I found a new "cee-ment pond". I did finally stop doing it, but it was years before I could even guess why this was happening.

It may have been that nothing had been added to this cement. Maybe it had been contaminated by dirt in the area or maybe it was left over at the end of the day and they just poured out that small amount to start fresh in the morning with a new mixture. Or maybe the amount of catalyst that was added was wrong and caused it to harden improperly. That may have been why they poured it out in the first place.

In any case, I never got my turtle right back then. I suppose I could find a professionally molded concrete turtle in a nursery, but there are other animals I'd rather collect for a garden at this time. I have already acquired a deer family, a rabbit, a squirrel, a chipmunk next to a stump, which is a flowerpot, and some mice and raccoons. Some of these are plastic and filled with sand, most are resin-cast and solid.

A number of years ago, my brother was mixing cement to sink some poles into the ground to make a dog-run for his hunting hounds. (How do you make a dog run? Show him a skunk?) As he turned the muck over in the wheelbarrow with a shovel to get a thorough blend, I told him, "I used to collect this stuff when we first moved here, and mold turtles out of it!"

He gave me a weird look, and slightly exasperated, asked, "Do you remember everything you've ever done?"

Well, yeah, doesn't everybody?

He still shakes his head at me often.

32. Learning to Ride a Bike

I had a tricycle for the first six years of my life. I remember it well. It was probably a hand-me-down, like most other larger items of its kind, having been used by all three brothers and my sister over the years. Maybe this one wasn't used by all of them; I don't know how long it had been around. But it was my main vehicle for years.

It was a small one in a dark blue color with an orange seat. Not a bright orange like road cones, and not a soft peach as I might have liked, but a sort of rusty butterscotch pudding color. It was painted in a smooth, shiny, thick enamel that almost made it look candy-coated.

I also remember that we had a larger red tricycle for bigger kids, and I remember my brother using it, but I don't know if I ever graduated to the big one. I'm not even sure if we brought it to California from Kansas when we moved. But my blue and orange one did make the trip.

Everyone my age was already riding bicycles in the new neighborhood, and it seemed a little strange that I would still be holding on to my tricycle. We moved to California the month before I turned 7, and less than three months before we would have our first Christmas in the new state, and in a freshly-built house.

The Sears Christmas catalog was always a favorite volume to pore over, and I would look through it for hours, day after day. The Dennis the Menace comics sprinkled throughout were an added entertainment as we would do our dreaming before Christmas, looking at the many items therein.

I had looked at a blue vehicle in the catalog that was called a "Super Sonda Scooter". It seemed to be a bike, but kind of a bulky one made to look something like a motorcycle. I thought it had pedals like a bike, but now I'm not sure, considering the name implied that you had to run your foot along the ground. I think that may have been just a fancy name to make it sound cool, but I couldn't tell you for sure at this time.

There was also a red bike in there, but since my best friend in the neighborhood had a blue one, and the girl most disliked on our street had a red one, I was more likely to stick with blue. I only made my preferences known and let my parents decide which one to get.

I did get a blue bike that Christmas, not the Super Sonda Scooter, but a more practical, traditional style bicycle that would probably last longer and fit my needs better. It was made by Royce Union, which was a brand I had never heard of. About 4 years later, I bought a bigger bike on my birthday, and it was the same brand, besides also being blue.

With that first bike, I definitely needed help learning to balance. I was used to three wheels that I didn't even need to think about as I sped down the sidewalk. On this one, I had training wheels to start with, and spent many a session later with my dad running behind me, trying to explain how to stay up on two wheels.

I thought I would never grasp the technique. Several times, my dad would take off the training wheels and hold on to the back until I was up and going. As soon as he'd let go, I was crashed on my side.

Once he stopped and tried to give me some detailed instructions. They went right over my head, and I replied, "Uh-uh". He looked a little exasperated as if he could see it was going to be a long drawn-out series of lessons.

Each time I would go through another attempt to solo, always winding up on my side in the street, I would ask either my dad or my brother to put the training wheels back on for awhile. This happened at least three times, and I was sure I was destined to have them on forever.

Finally, one of the times my brother put them on, he didn't let me know that he was raising them up a little higher so they wouldn't be on the ground. I'm still not sure if he did that on purpose, or if he put them on loosely so they raised when I rode on them. In any case, I was zooming around one afternoon, when one of the kids on my street yelled out, "hey, Theresa, your training wheels are off the ground! You're riding without them!"

I didn't believe it, and looked back. Seeing the wheels splayed out in the air, I promptly fell off.

But I knew that if I had been riding around like that without knowing it all that time, it probably meant I could balance, as long as I didn't think about it. I asked my brother to take them off, and they never went back on.

Later in that day, my brother was sitting on top of the slide in our backyard, looking over the fence as I continued to ride around. I didn't know he was watching me, and I didn't find out until later that he had my dad and my other brother with him when he made this evaluation of my newly learned skill:

"I didn't think the little punk would ever be able to do it!"

Such confidence from my big brother was always so inspiring. Still, everybody thought it was a funny line, and it was repeated in several letters to old friends in Kansas.

I did have some trouble with the various bikes I had over the years. Balancing wasn't the only problem to overcome. One day I was out riding around, and a somewhat older boy in the neighborhood was doing the same. This kid was known for blowing up over nothing and fighting people whenever he could.

As we were circling around in the street, he suddenly headed for me and purposely ran into me, knocking me off violently into the street. He fell off his own bike in the process. All of that was bad enough, but the next thing I knew, he came at me angrily, and punched me hard in both eyes.

A lady who lived two houses away from us was out in her front yard and witnessed the whole thing. She yelled at him that it was his own fault because he had deliberately run into me. I think she may have come over to help me since I wasn't seeing very well by then. She either walked me home, and explained to my parents what had happened or she may have called them later.

Another time, an older boy that I didn't know was riding with his girlfriend on the back of his bike and ran straight into me. They were both nice, and helped me up, making sure I wasn't too badly hurt.

This wasn't quite the case with a girl I ran into later. She was trying to get back on a bike that was too big for her, and I clumsily clipped her bike while I was trying to get around her. I had never seen her before, and didn't know if she even lived in the neighborhood. We both fell slightly, but caught ourselves.

"Guy, Girl," she said disgustedly. "What a dope!"

Once, I was out riding by myself, about a year or so after I'd mastered the technique. I thought it would be fun to experiment with something. I quickly moved my handlebars back and forth as I rode down the street. It wasn't long before I found myself on the ground with a very nice and stylish purple fingernail that throbbed and lasted a long time. I never tried that again.

Years later, when I was a teenager, I went to several schools that were out of my area. They were too far for me to ride my bike there, but there were buses in the area that went within blocks of the buildings I needed to attend. The bus stops, however, were not real close to home, and I would have been pooped if I had tried to walk to them every morning. Riding my bike, however, was a different story.

My mom had discovered that a certain gas station right near my bus stops had a number of bicycles locked to a rail in the back by the bathrooms. She asked the manager at the gas station if I could do the same. He gave her the go-ahead.

And so, I would ride to the gas station in the morning, lock up my bike, cross the busiest main street in the area and get my bus. In the afternoon, I would get off the bus at the stop right in front of the gas station, get my bike and go home.

It got kind of boring riding straight along the various small streets in our neighborhood on the way to the busy streets. So after awhile, I started cutting through the park at the end of our street.

There was a long walkway that wove through the park. One end was at the back of the park, which was closer to our house. That part of the park had been added a few years after the rest of it was built. The other end of the walkway was at the original front entrance parking lot around the corner on the next street.

The walkway ran between grassy areas and past the baseball field. Along one side of the park was a long fence that separated the park from all of the backyards of the houses along the street. Large evergreens had been planted, and there was a sort of musty dirty area around them, extending to the fence.

I found that a small group of boys, around junior high or early high school age would hang out under the trees with their backs against the fence. There were only about three or four of them. I never was sure if they had cut school or if they got out before I could get done with my bus ride. Since their schools were probably local, they may have had time to get to the park before I started my journey back from the gas station.

Being somewhat heavy in my mid to late teens, I was often the target of anti-fat comments. At this time, the favorite phrase of these local shade hounds seemed to be "Rent-a-Whale!"

I had ridden into the park one day, in time to see just one boy that I didn't know, coming out on his bike. He was the first to shout this clever phrase at me. I had no idea what he was talking about. I had never heard of such a thing, and wondered if it was just something he and his friends had come up with. It was only later that I was bombarded repeatedly with this strange statement by the group hanging out under the trees. I never did find out who they were, or if this original kid was one of them.

I never knew which trees they'd be under or if they'd even be there from day to day. Only after I had headed partway up the winding walkway could I be sure if this was their day to harass people. I was always ready.

"Rent-a-Whale! Rent-a-Whale!" the chorus would start up. Invariably, I would turn slightly to my right and answer, "What else did you learn in kindergarten today?"

"Nice *ass!*" they would reply, confirming my assessment of their maturity.

Clearly, the heavy shade back by the fence was affecting their eyesight. Or maybe they were just desperate. I came to expect this every day, and almost missed it when the time was over for me to ride through this way.

I never heard that phrase again from anyone else. It must have been a clique thing with them, or maybe others at their school who used it didn't live in the area. Later when I rode my bike, and then my moped to work, I used to pass by a slightly beat up white car parked in front of a house that had a business name, "Rent-a-Wreck" printed on a sticker on the back bumper. I always wondered if one of the kids from the park lived in that house.

33. How Much Faith Does it Take to Pierce a Rock?

I had heard of miracles. I knew they happened. And I knew they could still happen...

One thing we had in abundance when we moved to the new place was rocks. They were everywhere. Rocks showed up in all shapes and sizes, with a wide range of shades of grey, black, tan, chocolate brown, etc. I would check them out, not only in our own yard but in the empty lots nearby. At one time, I had read a book about a kid who had some rocks and someone discovered there was amethyst inside when they broke them open. I took to picking up rocks and throwing them hard in the street to bust them apart. No luck.

One day I did find a rock near our house that seemed to be a red color with some white running through it. I thought it looked like a small steak. I discovered that it had a strange shape broken out of it, and later found a piece nearby that fit into the broken area. I took both pieces inside, washed them thoroughly and glued them back together. I'm pretty sure it's still around the house somewhere, along with my fudge rock that I got at school years later, and the baked potato rock which we had brought from Kansas. They're probably packed somewhere.

While walking home from the school bus stop in second or third grade, I discovered a fairly large green rock in one of the empty lots which was waiting for a house to be built on it. The rock was a little too big and heavy for me; about the size of a beef roast or a small watermelon. A boy from my class, who lived up the street from me offered to bring it home for me. When we got home, my mom happened to be in the front yard, and thanked my friend for bringing it home. I still don't know if she was being sarcastic, or if she was really glad that I could get someone to help me. We kept the rock under the drainpipe on the corner of the garage for years.

That same kid was invited to one of my birthday parties. I always did hang out more with boys than girls. I believe he gave me a Flipper paint-by-number set, complete with water colors for filling in the various dolphin scenes. Another boy from the neighborhood gave me a set of fancy soaps in the shape of fruit. I think there were two yellow pears, a bunch of purple grapes, a strawberry, a lime and a lemon. He had no way of knowing that many years later, I would become an incredible out-of-control fruit freak, collecting everything I could find with pictures of fruit or items in the shape of fruit. The soaps were just the beginning, but I used them at the time, so I didn't have them by the time I started collecting other stuff.

I had picked up another rock one day, a large, black stone about the size of a large orange or small grapefruit. It wasn't shaped like one though. It was slightly flattened, like a very thick steak, and had a lot of peaks and valleys in it. I didn't know what I was going to do with it, but it seemed like such a nice, rich black, I didn't want to just throw it back.

One night, I decided to prove to everyone that miracles were indeed possible. I didn't tell them exactly what I was doing; I thought they'd be able to figure it out once I set everything up. I decided to get a hole to appear through the rock without any carving or drilling on my part. What I did was, I put the rock on the kitchen table and laid my biggest rosary around it. I knew, beyond everything, that there was power from God capable of making a hole appear in there, if I left it long enough.

It wasn't destined to stay there very long though. Within the first hour or so, somebody asked me what I was doing. I told them I was trying to get a hole to appear through the rock, from one side to the other. I didn't have any real reason to want a hole there; It was certainly too big to hang around my neck, and would have given me a quick headache. I was just trying to prove that I had faith.

My family didn't understand what the rosary had to do with anything, and I didn't think I needed to explain. It seemed that since they had taught me about miracles, they should know what I was trying to do.

My dad, at some point, started laughing. He thought he had figured it out. He asked if I was trying to make the rock holey by putting a blessed item around it. I got mad, even though it was an innocent question, as he thought I was misunderstanding the word, "holy". When I couldn't explain it to them, I gave up and took the whole display away.

But I knew all along, and since, that it was still possible. If He had wanted a hole in that rock, He would have put one there. He wasn't the one who had to prove anything, certainly not to me, and my family wasn't ready to see it.

That is when I knew for sure that it is His will that is to be done, not ours. And who knows? Maybe that rock went back into our yard, and someone will dig it up someday – and discover holes all through it.

34. Eyeing the Girls

When I was in third grade, there was a kid in one of the other third grade classes named Steve. Though I didn't know most of the kids in the other classes, I somehow managed to learn a lot of their names. This was accomplished, either by listening hard at recess, talking to kids I knew who happened to know these other kids or hearing stories about a particular talent or handicap one had.

Because of the ugly, ancient practice of gossip, it was often easy to find out things about someone without meeting the person. If someone had an attribute that was a bit different, the word would spread.

Sometimes we would find out something about someone by way of our teacher. This happened in the case of a kid who was in my brother's class, three years ahead of us. A kid named Lenny had a rare bone disease that caused him to be unusually skinny. I never did know what it was. I hadn't even noticed him until our teacher pointed out to our class one day that she had overheard some kids teasing him, calling him names like "String Bean". Our teacher let us know at that time, that if she ever caught any of us making fun of him, we would be in severe trouble.

That was the only way I learned this kid's name, or managed to figure out later who he was. And, as it turned out, a physical defect was also the only way I happened to learn Steve's name.

And what was Steve's unique trait? Simply that he had a glass eye. I never did find out why, or what happened to the real thing, but word spread quickly that one of his eyes wasn't real.

As it turned out, there was more than one way to find this out. First, there was the aforementioned gossip that spread around the school like wildfire. And the second method made me glad I wasn't in the same class with him, and therefore wouldn't tempt him to try his games on me.

For Steve seemed to derive great pleasure in taking his eye out at recess and chasing the girls around the playground with it in his outstretched hand. At times, I would be sitting on the bench outside the classroom, or just walking around with a friend, and I would suddenly be startled by the sound of shrieking young females. I would look up and see a crowd of girls from the other class running away from a boy who had thrust his arm fully in front of himself. In his hand would be one of his eyes. On his face, and in the remaining eye, a menacing and satisfied look would be throwing its beams into the mass of terrified girls.

Years later, when I mentioned this at home, my mother wondered if his mother knew what he was doing for fun, flaunting this expensive item with which his parents had provided him. She pointed out that his mother probably would have been horrified, had she known.

Like I said, I was gratified he wasn't in my class and didn't know me. Each time I'd see this starting up on the playground, I'd sit back in amusement and observe this early and unusual form of girl watching he'd invented.

35. I've Gone to Pot at Age 8

In my own third grade class there was a boy who I did know, unlike Steve the glass-eyed kid, and I couldn't stand him. I don't remember exactly why – it wasn't a normal case of "yucky boys" or "cootie fears". I had always gotten along with boys, sometimes better than I did with the girls. But there was something about this kid, Danny Scott, which I couldn't take at all. For this reason, I referred to him as Danny Pot, as in toilet. I didn't know anything about hallucinogenic drugs at that time.

Being eight years old, the others in my class understood what I meant when I referred to him as "Pot". Some of the other girls giggled with me about it, and used that name whenever they'd talk about him around me. It seemed to be fitting, as some of the other girls thought he was a creep also.

All this, however, didn't mean I should go out of my way to harass him, but I couldn't resist it. A couple of incidents come to mind, one of which was completely impulsive and the other planned to work out the way it did.

The first thing I remember doing to him involved water in the classroom. Like many of the lower grade classrooms, we had a sink with a drinking fountain attached to it, installed in the corner of the room. We used it when we had art classes that were messy and required the washing of hands and/or desks, and we may have had to wash our hands before lunch. The drinking fountain was there for convenience, so we wouldn't have to go outside to the corridors or playground, wherever they had the bigger ones installed.

One day, I was in desperate need of a drink, (water would do, though something stronger might have been nice), and I went over to the small drinking fountain at our classroom sink. As many kids do, I took a long swig and held it in my cheeks like a hamster gathering food. When

I turned away, I really did plan to hold it there until I got back to my desk and then swallow it. I really, really did! But Danny Scott just sat too close to the drinking fountain to pass up the opportunity.

Impulsively, I let go of my reservoir of liquid, spurting it right in his face. He wasn't looking up when I did it, but he did later, as he emitted a loud protest.

I got in trouble that time, but I thought it was worth it. Good thing I've gotten over that kind of thinking, and have turned into a model for raising your kids!

The second time I remember doing something to him, I don't believe I got caught. But I was a bit remorseful later anyway.

Each year at that school, they held a Christmas play and a Spring Festival. No class was involved in both programs in the same year – they alternated. If you were in the Christmas play one year, you were in the Spring Festival the next year. I was only at that school for two years. In second grade, I was a toy horse, brought by Santa Claus in the Christmas play. My neighbor was Santa Claus. There were four of each toy, and each group had a verse of a song to sing to the audience. My group sang,

> Oh, I'm a walking horsie
> With reins and a saddle too
> When you sit on me right
> I move like horses do!

We each had to get stick horses so we could ride up to the edge of the stage before singing, and ride back to the rest of the toys when we were finished. Some of the kids borrowed horses from their younger siblings. I had to go out and buy one. As it turned out, when I went to get mine, the only thing available was a zebra. It was called, "Zee Bee". I had to use it. I'm not sure the audience could see the details on it anyway.

In third grade, we played song flutes in the spring festival. At the beginning of the year, or maybe shortly after, each of the third grade teachers passed out the plastic flutes to their students. Our teacher told us there would be a few rules. One I remember distinctly. Anyone caught playing a stray note on their own, outside of the practice sessions with the class would have to miss the rest of that practice session. They would have to put their flute away in their desk, and just sit listening to everybody else. She didn't want to create a chaotic zoo-like environment with everyone tooting here and there.

This was too good. I knew, from past experiences with whistles, and experience with my flute when I took it home, that if you cover the large slot that you blow past, there will be no sound. You could easily pretend to blow a note, and wind up with just a light, airy noise that wouldn't be heard far. I would keep that thought in mind for later.

One of our favorite things to hear from our teacher was, "take out your flutes". I'm not sure it was at the same time or on the same day each week. We did seem to be pleasantly surprised when we'd hear it, so maybe she just worked it in between other regular subjects. We all looked forward to the time spent practicing in the classroom.

I would sometimes see my teacher sitting at the piano in our room, figuring out the notes we were to play. That's when I knew we'd be getting a new song. In the beginning, we had short songs like "Mary Had a Little Lamb", or we would learn notes we hadn't gone over before. After an hour or so, we would put away or flutes and be given an assignment to practice at home.

My entire family, especially my brothers, got tired of hearing "Mary Had a Little Lamb" all the time. One of my brothers, who had been playing the trumpet and other instruments for awhile, threatened to play something I hated if I kept playing that song. I don't remember what it was. I do remember purposely playing "Mary Had a Little Lamb" to annoy one of my other brothers and he called our older brother's name. I don't think he was home, or he didn't hear. I do remember stopping immediately so I wouldn't have to hear whatever it was that was threatened.

Not long after we started learning this instrument in my class, I asked my teacher where to get a flute I could use at home, instead of bringing the school's instrument home every time. She told me about a music store in our then downtown shopping center, and said they cost one dollar. My mom took me there, and I got my own, which I could use anytime, and keep after I'd left that school.

One day, we heard the welcome command, "take out your flutes". We all scrambled in our desks to retrieve them. Danny Scott sat in the row next to mine at this time, and a few seats behind the one across from me.

While we were preparing for our lesson, I had another attack of impishness, not unlike the water incident. I turned toward him with my flute in my lips, secretly covered the slot, and blew hard. Only the light airy sound came out.

Danny Scott's eyes got big. "How'd you do that?" he exclaimed.

He immediately picked up his flute and blew a loud note into the classroom. Our teacher followed the sound, caught Danny with his flute up to his mouth, and made him put it away.

A few minutes later, after we had started playing as a group, I looked back and caught a very unhappy look on Danny's face. He may have even been glaring at me along with it, but he may have been looking down at his desk; I don't remember. I had a fleeting bit of remorse, because I knew I had caused this, but I was also a bit gleeful. Still, I knew it wasn't nice.

After I left that school, I continued with the Camp Fire group there, because the school I went to didn't have one.

They only had Girl Scouts. Sometime in that next year, one of the girls in that group, who had been my best friend at the other school, informed me at a Camp Fire meeting, "Danny Pot broke his leg". She added, "He fell in the toilet!"

I don't think that was how it really happened. But she seemed to know it would get a giggle out of me. Like I said, she wasn't crazy about him either. And she knew just what to say to connect with me.

36. No, Really - What's For Dessert?

"What's for dessert?" has been heard around households for generations. At our house, for many years, the answer was the same: "cookies or ice cream". Or on special occasions, there might be cake or pie. In our first two years or so of living in a house built in an old cherry orchard, there were also many offers of cherry cobbler. Since I never could stand hot fruit, and I wasn't crazy about the variety of cherries that had ended up being in the yard of the lot my parents had picked, I often declined this, after trying it once or twice.

Starting in about second or third grade, my immediate answer to "what's for dessert?" proclaimed in front of the entire family was, "barfed up dirt!"

The word "barf" had been introduced to me, mainly by MAD magazine. This was one of my favorite forms of reading material, which I had first heard of through my brothers. It remained at the top of my reading list for many years. Informative! Educating! Wholesome and edifying! I learned a lot from these guys, mostly grossly represented information. And I *do* mean grossly!

Therefore, "barf" became my favorite word for a long time. When I worked for a now well-known computer company as my first job, (a very much *unknown* company at the time), I would often type in the word as my name when playing video games on my break or at home. Only, in that case, I usually spelled it with a double 'r'. People would often walk in on me to find me addressed by the machine as, "Space Pilot Trainee Barrf", "Captain Barrf", "Major Barrf", etc. Although, sometimes I would give myself other names so I could work up to "Captain Crunch", "Captain Kangaroo", "Major Problem" and others of that kind.

Also, in another game we had on that machine, the player was instructed ahead of time to pick a "self-destruct password". That way, if things went badly in the game, you didn't have to wait for the computer to beat the guts out of you; instead you could press a key that prompted the words, "enter self-destruct password". After I would type in "Barrf" the screen would flash at me several times, making boinging noises in time with the flash, and a letter would appear on the screen, notifying my next-of-kin that my ship had been blown up. How nice.

In later years, I was amazed that I hadn't come up with other answers to similar questions about food. Why stop at dessert? Only after I stopped to think about this a few years ago, did I come up with these rhymes:

> *What are we gonna eat?*
> *Rotten meat!*
> <u>*What*</u> *are we gonna eat?*
> *Dirty feet!*
> *What's for breakfast?*
> *Special dreck–fest!*
> *What's for lunch?*
> *Nibble & munch!*
> *What's for dinner?*
> *Unrepentant sinner!*
> *What's for dessert?*
> *Barfed up dirt!*

The possibilities were endless. Still, they never occurred to me until we started having other kids around the table who I was warned not to influence with such behavior. First it was a niece, then a nephew, a great-niece or two, etc. I probably would have been slaughtered right after the meal if I'd done that. Or else halfway through the meal, before dessert. That would have been the worst cruelty.

This is not to say I haven't been provoked recently to reintroduce my poetry. Oftentimes, my oldest brother will wait for just the right time, look at me impishly and ask, "What's for dessert?"

Rather than blurt it loudly as before, my reply has usually been, "mrfdpdrt!"

37. Knowing Who Your Marbles Are

Orbs of glass... Spheres of hard, breakable stuff in many colors and sizes… Lots of people collect them. Some companies even advertise on them. Kids play with them – adults sometimes display them. But can they tell them apart if they don't have someone's advertising logo on them? Sure, there may be slightly different colors, swirls, different arrangement of the colored pieces inside the clear part. But what if they had names? Marbles, they're called, and that's where I treat them differently than others. I name them.

It all started in second or third grade. One Sunday morning, I was ready for church earlier than the rest of my family, so I went out in the front yard for a few minutes. Standing out in the grass, I noticed something in my next door neighbors' front yard. One of their kids had hidden about thirty marbles in the grass. They were peeking out all over in different colors.

The kid next door, who was my age, saw me eyeing the items in his grass. I think he might have been afraid I'd collect them and make off with them. He came out to talk with me.

This kid was into making deals. He often had driveway sales of toys he didn't want anymore, and sometimes let his little brother put things in for sale too. It was their way of making money for new toys they wanted. Once they had a sale that consisted mostly of balloons and the little brother's Gumby doll. When I asked how much things were being sold for, the two-year-old answered, "Forty-ten dollars!" His older brother said, "No they're not!" The little one insisted, "Well, Gumby is!" He wanted to make sure he made enough off this deal. After all, Gumby's arms *were* pre-chewed! That must have taken a lot of work on his part.

So here we were, alone in our front yards on a Sunday morning, and Tom realized he had something I was interested in. He started talking to me about selling me all the marbles in the grass. He estimated the number of marbles, figured an amount for the lot, which ended up being more than they cost in the store at the time, and made me the offer. I quickly ran into the house, emptied change from my bank and bought the marbles. Tom helped me pick them out of the grass.

Immediately after making my purchase, I went into the house and received a lecture about how I shouldn't be buying things off the neighbor kids. Then, just before we all left for church, I was given a small cloth drawstring bag my mom had made years before, which contained marbles previously belonging to my oldest brother. I added them to my new collection. It wasn't long before I had about 100 of them.

I don't remember what started me doing this, but I named every one of those marbles after people I knew. Most were from school, but some were from the neighborhood and family too. At that time, I used to take them swimming every night in the bathtub. Sometimes I would have them race in the bathtub. I would push them all up to one end, hold them there with my arm for awhile and then let go. I had no idea what this sounded like downstairs. Every night, my family had to listen to the rumble of 100 marbles rolling from one end of the bathtub to the other. As if this weren't bad enough to subject them to, I had to have diving practice as well! One by one, the marbles would roll off the faucet and into the tub. Clunk! Clunk! Clunk! After awhile, they'd clunk against each other. That must have sounded good.

Near the end of my third grade year, one of our neighbors was transferred to Australia. Their kids were told they had to give a lot of their toys away; they couldn't take a bunch of stuff with them. Since my brother hung around a lot with one of their kids, he ended up getting most of what Mickey had to get rid of. One of the things Mickey gave him was a shrunken head. I don't know if it was real. It was ugly; a strange shade of green-brown with a string through its nose and long, stiff black hair. My brother used to carry it around by its hair, which stuck straight back from the back of its head, and say, "I used to smoke, but not anymore!"

Another thing Mickey gave my brother was an orange plastic beach pail that was filled to the top with marbles. I was awestruck. I had never seen that many marbles. My brother kept them in his closet and would only let me see them every once in awhile. When he wanted me out of his room, it was the end of visiting hours.

Then one Christmas, I was told my brother had a special gift for me. I couldn't believe it. Even though I had always made sure I had something for everybody, my sister was the only one of the siblings who ever gave me anything. My brothers never even thought about it back then.

On this Christmas, my brother went upstairs and came down with his bucket of marbles. He presented me with the whole thing. There were 643 of them. I went to work naming them right away.

Even though a lot of them have distinguishing marks if you look closely enough, many of them are hard to tell apart. So I had to put them in separate containers depending on where I knew the people from. One of the schools I went to is in a tortilla chip can. Another school is in an apple juice bottle. A couple of other groups are in plastic bags. A few people from a company I worked at are in cigar tubes.

Some people save photographs to remember people. I save marbles. What can I say? This is also a great memory exercise, as there is no place on a marble to write a person's name, as there is on the back of a photo.

Because there are a lot that look somewhat alike, there is another tradition I've started. Each marble that is named also bears the name of the first person who that type of marble was named after. For instance, a red Chinese-checker type marble would be known as a "Christie Howard type" because she was the first person to have that kind of marble named for her. When I'm showing a marble of that type to someone, which happens to be named for someone else, I mainly let the person know who that marble is for. But in my head, I know it's a Christie Howard type, and I may explain that to others after they've seen more of my marbles, or asked about them. Sometimes people want to know why I picked a certain one for a particular person. It may be that it's the color I've seen them wear the most. Once in awhile, a marble just looks like somebody – no particular reason. Sometimes the swirls look like the person's hair. Sometimes there is a color that is associated with them because of something they've been involved in, like red, white and blue for a patriotic person. I also have a few marbles that are named for people I never really knew; they just happened to be good friends of somebody else, so I picked one that looked like that person, and let them have a friend in the bag with them. In one case, it turned out that a person had the same initials as one of the earlier-named ones of her type. However, I didn't notice that until later. I had merely named the second one because I knew she had pants that color. I was amazed later on when I realized they had similar names.

I've kept up this hobby ever since second or third grade, when I started it, and though I don't have one for everybody I've ever met, (as some people seem to think), I do have several hundred named and many unnamed. I keep the unnamed ones in a small overnight case that was my sister's many years ago. That's where I go fishing and searching when I want to name a new one. Besides the first 100 and the next 643, I also have some I've found in the street and others I've bought at various stores over the years. Usually the ones found in the street are named for the person whose house it was in front of, even if it was on a corner and may have rolled from somewhere else. I always figured if I was going to steal it from the person, the least I could do is name it after them! People may sometimes wonder why I'd buy more when I have so many unnamed ones, but sometimes there is just a certain thing that seems to fit a person, and I don't have it. I've been known to buy a whole bag just to get one that is perfect for somebody. I usually end up naming others from the bag, but I always remember that the bag was bought for a certain person.

In later years, when I had been driving for awhile, I had a custom bumper sticker made. In large block letters, it states, "I KNOW WHO ALL MY MARBLES ARE." I've been asked about it on the street, and sometimes after I've explained, I'm not sure if the people wish they hadn't asked, or if they even get it. I've gotten some strange, blank looks. Some have laughed at it without asking or knowing anything about me. Others who know me have gotten it right away.

One hot day, when I still had my old car, I was driving along a busy street in a nearby town. My air conditioner had blitzed on me sometime earlier; the cooling part still worked, but the fan didn't blow anymore. I had to make do on hot days by turning on the AC button and opening side windows to let air circulate through the fan and from one side of the car to the other. Therefore, I was driving along in fairly heavy traffic with my windows mostly open.

I stopped at a red light in the second lane, and noticed cars in the far right lane moving ahead as they made right turns when safe. As they crept ahead, passing me up, I heard a heavily-accented voice slowly reading, "I – know - who - all - my –marbles - are."

I quickly looked out the other window, away from the right lane. There was no way I was going to explain that to someone who probably wouldn't get it anyway. I'd probably miss my green light and get a lot of people mad at me, besides getting weird looks from the guy in the next lane. Better to roll along, closer to home where my marbles were. They were the ones who knew me and would understand.

38. Must Be that Dairy Air!

When my brother was in sixth grade, he had a teacher he didn't like much. Her name was Mrs. Scandy. I was never sure why he didn't like her, and didn't get a chance to find out, since I never got her for a teacher. All I knew was that he would come home from school saying rude things about her in a grumpy voice. Mostly it involved something about her resemblance to something bovine.

Lunch recess was always an important part of the day, especially after getting the eating part done with. Can't waste that extra recess time with something as petty as food! We had to get to the playing as soon as possible.

One day, I was walking back from the cafeteria with 2 friends from my class, Jean & Kathy. We had ended the "food" part of lunch, and were heading toward the playground for the important part. We decided to walk through the outdoor corridor between two rows of classrooms. As we passed the sixth grade room, Mrs. Scandy was standing at the door, either locking up her classroom so she could go to lunch, or unlocking it so she could go inside.

I turned to my friends, informing them in a not-too-quiet voice, "My brother says she looks like a cow!"

Mrs. Scandy turned around, flashing a big smile, as my friends, Kathy and Jean, laughing, punched me in the arm and shushed me.

I've often wondered if she knew who my brother was. And if she knew I was referring to her. It must have been a very moo-ving experience.

Reminds me of a book I found in my brother's room one day. It was an old textbook, not being used by the school anymore, and had been discarded, either having been passed out to whatever kids wanted them or sold at a rummage sale. It seemed to be a science book, possibly for the fourth or fifth grade. One day, while flipping through it, I found a comment that had been added by a former student of one of the teachers at that same school.

The page I ran across had pictures of three mice in various stages of growth. Clearly it was some kind of experiment on these lab animals; maybe it was described on one of the nearby pages, but I didn't check it out. What I noticed though, was the addition scrawled in pen. Across the biggest and fattest mouse, someone had added the words, "Mrs. Peterson".

Funny, I didn't remember her being fat, or bearing any resemblance to a rodent. It could only be the comment of another disgruntled student, like my brother's reference to Mrs. Scandy's girth, which I didn't see myself either.

Did my brother ever have good teachers? I think so. I do remember the teacher he had in fifth grade, Mrs. Wright, who always had something good to write on his report card. That must have been a better year for him. And he did sometimes have good things to say about her. She must have been the Wright teacher for the job.

39. I'm Pool Guy, the Everything Man! (Toot! Toot!)

Everybody's heard of Avon. Seems they've been around forever. I don't know their exact date of establishment, but I suspect that Eve sold fig leaf polish and preservative.

I remember their commercials from when I was very small. I don't think they advertise on TV anymore, but I know they used to. I became very familiar with the "Ding-dong! Avon calling!" followed by the spiel, which I don't remember because I stopped listening at that point. But I still remember the voice.

I was mistaken for an Avon lady once when I was about sixteen. The father of a girl in my school owned a print shop, and would sometimes make work available for the students to earn extra money for the school, delivering flyers or sometimes note pads with advertising on them. He'd supply the items to be delivered and specify the neighborhood for us to take them.

The day we had the note pads, I stocked up on a large supply for the street I was assigned to. It was easier for me to carry more because I normally brought my lunch to school in a two-toned blue fabric tote bag with flowers on it. It made the perfect carrying case for the small pads, which probably bore the name of a real estate agent. I moved my lunch aside and stacked as many note pads as I could in the tote bag.

I was going along at a nice pace, throwing the pads on the front step of each house and moving on to the next house. After a few, I noticed a small boy, maybe three years old, sitting on his tricycle in front of one house.

"Why you didn't throw me one?" he asked me.

I told him I was just putting them at the houses. He pondered that a bit, then jumped off his tricycle and ran up to the last house where I'd been, retrieving the pad I had left there. Fine with me – maybe he lived there, or the occupants would have thrown it away anyway. My work was done, and the kid had something to color on.

Further down the road, I walked up a driveway past a pickup truck parked, and, unknown to me, occupied by a somewhat grizzly looking man. As I passed the truck on the way to the door, I heard a voice boom out, "hello, Avon lady!"

I thought he was joking, so I handed him a note pad from my bag. "My wife has one in the house," he said without reaching for it.

I wondered who had gotten there first. I was sure my schoolmates had gone to other streets, fanning out to cover the area quicker. The guy must have seen the confused look on my face, for he said, "Aren't you the Avon lady?"

"No," I said.

"What are you?"

What am I? I'm a sixteen-year-old trying to make money for my school! Do I look like I'm selling cosmetics? Do I reek of Sweet Honesty? To him I answered haltingly, "Um, I'm just passing these out."

He took a closer look. "Oh," he said, taking it.

Well, I'm glad that's over! What am I? Taken aback, that's what!

Years earlier, however, I was glad to see the Avon lady. In Kansas, we bought often; In California, it seemed we bought less, but did get regular visits once we had met the lady assigned to our area. And one item I remember the most was The Everything Man.

This was not an official Avon name for the product. It's only what I named my first one and every one I received after that. At least 4 in all, I believe. This was a product known as First Mate's Shampoo, which came in a bottle shaped like a roly-poly sailor with his hand to his ear. The cap to the bottle was a sailor cap which screwed on and off easily. That would explain why I often lost his hat.

His pants were blue, but not navy blue; closer to turquoise or deep sky blue. His shirt was white, his tie, shoes and the pupils of his eyes were black. The whites of his eyes blended into the snowy white of his skin, making me think for years that he had little beady black eyes. But if you looked close, the indentations in the face where the eyes went were molded clearly.

I decided this was my jack-of-all-trades, though I really didn't know at the time that there was such a thing. This was just someone who knew how to do everything for me, so I named him The Everything Man. "He does everything for you," is how I explained it to others, at least those I would talk to. Once in awhile, one of the ladies present at the time would make a subtle, faintly dirty, joke by saying, "he's not *my* everything man!" and giggling with her cohorts. At age six, this went right over my head.

After awhile, I worked out a deal with him. In the evenings, while taking a bath, I would spend a lot of time playing in there before getting out. Making soapsuds was a major thrill, even though it did dry my skin out. The thicker the suds, the better I was. Sometimes I would have a pitcher in there with me, and I would fill it most of the way with water, topping it off with thick suds. This was my secret beer recipe, and, it turned out, the best beer The Everything Man had ever tasted. He, in turn had come up with a great formula for swimming pool chlorine which was the best around. We made a deal - if I would leave him a whole pitcher of my beer, he'd leave me chlorine for my pool, which was the bathtub. The next night when I'd get in the bathtub, the suds would be gone from the pitcher, and it would be almost full of whitish slimy water. He must have been there. I'd pour the soapy sludge into my new bath and start over. I didn't think about the concentration of skin-drying soap or the bacteria that may have grown overnight. It was my favorite game.

Later I came up with a great pudding recipe, which was pure, thick soapsuds with as little water as possible in them. I'd leave him a cup of that, and he'd leave me his other formula, which was called cocoon chlorine. This was formed from the remnants of the soap as it dried overnight and through the next day. No matter how hard I tried, I could never get all the water out; there would always be a little bit in the bottom of the cup the next day. It was necessary for getting a good lather from the soap. But most of the cup would be crusted with the feathery-light dried bubbles, sometimes in a flat sheet over part of the top. This would be dissolved in my bath for my swimming students, which were my marbles, as explained in Chapter 37.

I was really into catching butterflies back then, and would often look for cocoons on the fence. I never saw one open up, even when I would pry one off with a stick and keep it in a jar. I only sometimes saw the ones on the fence after the insect was gone, and never got to see what was in there. I suspected they were for moths anyway. But I knew what the material of a cocoon looked like. And the dried soapsuds reminded me of that stuff. It wasn't chlorine, any more than my concoctions were beer or pudding, but that's the power of a kid's imagination. So, The Everything Man's invention was named Cocoon Chlorine.

As mentioned, I probably owned at least four of these sailor bottles over the years. One was taken to the public swimming pool in Kansas, and disappeared along with my brown-haired troll doll, which I had received when I got my tonsils out. I seem to remember bringing three items to the pool that day to play with, and leaving them for awhile in the overflow at the edge of the pool. I don't remember what the third item was, or if it vanished along with the others. And I'm still not sure if they were stolen, or just floated away.

I'm not sure if I threw one away when I got a new one or not. I do know that after playing with them awhile, especially in water, the blue coloring would scratch and wear off of his pants. Therefore, getting more shampoo was a good way to replace his ratty clothes. I know that I still had one after moving from Kansas to California, and that's the one I exchanged beer and pudding with for his special chlorine. But that one's been gone for years too.

I never knew the official Avon name of the product until about 15 years ago. I was in a bookstore and saw a book on collector's items, including a section on old Avon bottles & decanters. It included a lot of pictures. I kept looking until I saw my familiar old fat sailor holding up his hand to his ear. There was the item name, First Mate's Shampoo.

I looked around for years in antique shops, thrift stores, garage sales, etc. This was before ebay. Once that came about, I was able to search for it by name.

It took me awhile to find it, but one day, there it was. Not only did this person have The Everything Man, but it was full, unopened, and in its original box, which I had forgotten about. The box had goofy drawings of the sailor and a seabird of some sort. Once I saw that, I remembered it, including the silly expression and placement of the eyes on the drawing, which were not the same as on the bottle, but suggested possible seasickness. The seller also included some soap in the shape of an anchor, which may have been a part of their series at the time.

I was outbid on my first attempt, but was determined to get this, and I did. I saved the box, but wanted to display the sailor as I always had in the bathroom. At first he had his place on the corner of the bathtub as before, but later, in order to keep him dry and preserve the color, I removed him from that spot and placed him on top of a cabinet where I keep other bath items. Around him are five birds, one itself an Avon container, but the other four are salt and pepper shakers. I like to think that The Everything Man is finally retired, and feeding the birds now. And maybe wishing he could go for a swim in his own chlorine. But I wouldn't sit in that stuff now.

40. Invention of the Worm Maker

Where I got the plastic nozzle from a spray can, I'm not sure. I think maybe it came off an aerosol can of bug spray at home. But at nine years old, it was a fascinating thing to have. It was yellow, about a half inch long, and fun. I don't remember if I found it in the street; I seem to remember taking it off a can of something at home after the product ran out. I don't have it anymore, but they're easy enough to get if I have the urge to play again.

I carried it around for awhile, trying to think of something unique to use it for. Somewhere along the way, I believe within the first day I had it, I found a small screw in a drawer, and found that it fit into the larger hole in the bottom, where the tube from the can used to be. It was a little tight in there at first, but as I turned it, the soft plastic took on the shape of the screw threads, which shaved away a little plastic to make room.

I had a "thing" for modeling clay back then, and still do. I no longer use it to make candy for the innocent little neighbor kids to buy – I learned my lesson with that when I was seven or eight and got caught by my parents. But any time I could get anything even resembling clay, whether it was putty, the red wax off of the outside of edam cheese, thick white paste, etc., I would find a use for it. Even at this time, I have a big hunk of the red wax off cheese that is stuck to my bedroom floor from a time early this year or late last year when I collected a bunch and worked it in my hands. I didn't know it wound up on my floor, and it was covered for months by other items, so it got pretty flat and stuck by the time summer rolled around. I plan to scrape it up pretty soon.

Once I had my aerosol can nozzle fit nicely with the screw, I decided to put some clay in the hole and push it out through the smaller hole by slowly screwing the screw inward. When I did, a very thin, squiggling worm went flying out the hole in the front.

This was exciting!! For the rest of that evening, I continued smashing up the worm, reinserting it in the big hole and creating a new fast-wiggling, long skinny worm. I couldn't believe how much fun it was – and I had discovered it!

As a fourth grader in a Catholic school, part of my uniform was the blue sweater with the initials of the school name in a white circle on one side. I had forgotten about that until recently, when I went into a McDonald's on what was probably the last day of school before this past summer. While I was standing in line, a couple of small kids came in with their mother. They were wearing uniforms from that same school I had gone to for one year; white blouses, blue and grey plaid skirts and that sweater with the circle on it. I cringed. That place wasn't quite as bad as the Catholic school I went to for 4 years after that, but it wasn't the greatest place I've had to do time in, either.

I decided one day in fourth grade, to bring my toy to school. It fit nicely in my sweater pocket. Before recess, I loaded it with white paste – that thick, smelly stuff that came in a jar with either a brush or a flat stick built into the lid for spreading. I made sure it was some of the soft fresh stuff from the middle of the jar, rather than the crusty dried stuff from the edge.

Speaking of that kind of paste, which I haven't used for years, I remember various stories about it over the years. When I was in kindergarten, our teacher put a bunch of jars of this stuff on a table so we could all work on some kind of art project. I remember one girl wrinkling her nose at the smell and stating loudly, "This smells like my grandfather's after-shave!" I wondered what brand he used, and hoped nobody in my family would take up a liking for that brand.

Also, we met a girl a few years later, who was once asked by her teacher in school, "Why should we never eat paste?" Her answer: "Because it's made out of bug juice!"

Getting back to fourth grade, I went out to recess with my toy, and was either in the girls' bathroom or on the playground when I made a paste worm. Someone in my class immediately asked me, "What's that?"

Another girl in the class rolled her eyes good-naturedly and said, "Probably another one of her inventions!"

Hey, don't knock it! The company that made Play-Doh sold a lot of Funny Pumpers. And they could very well have come about because someone like me learned to fashion a Worm Maker.

41. Somebody's Gonna Need an Ambulance!

During my fourth grade year, the annual drawing of names for Christmas presents took place in early December. I always remember that the last day of school before Christmas that year was December 19th. I don't know why that stuck in my mind, but near the end of our vacation time, I remember saying to my brothers, "don't you wish it was still December 19th?"

I also remember that my parents went to Las Vegas shortly before Christmas that year. On the last day of school, I suffered with a toothache that had been going on for a few days, and by the end of the day, I had a swollen jaw. When I came out to the car at the end of the school day, my mom thought I had a piece of candy in my cheek from the school party. When I told her my tooth was still hurting, I ended up having to go to the dentist and have it pulled. My parents left for Vegas after that, and my sister had to take care of me and remind me to rinse with salt water every day.

Back to the gift exchange... I happened to pick a kid named Kurt, who I despised. I always thought he was dopey and dorky; the idea of having to buy him a present mortified me. Nevertheless, I went shopping with my mom before their trip, and ended up buying him a Matchbox ambulance.

Sometime between my wrapping of the gift, and his unwrapping, the words, "you're dumb" wound up being written on the back of the gift tag. I truly don't know how they got there. I swear to you, I didn't do it. To this day, I don't know if someone in my family wrote it on a card that hadn't been used yet, and I just happened to pick that one up to put on my gift, or if someone in my class was trying

146

to slander me. All I know is that Kurt noticed… and didn't like it one bit.

"What's this?" he asked me. I was as surprised as he was, but thought, "What's it look like?" He went on to say, "I don't like this." But I was baffled, and denied it all honestly.

Even if it was the truth.

42. Age Requirement
at the Post Office

I think it was Christmas time. Either that, or it was one of the rare times that my mom buckled down and wrote letters to everyone she'd known in the last 20 years. Nah, it must have been Christmas time. And I was about 11.

It was a day for errands, and one was to get a lot of stamps from the Post Office. I went along for the ride. After several other stops, the grocery store, cleaners, or whatever, we wound up at the Post Office downtown.

This was the only Post Office I knew of in our city at that time; later they built at least two others, one close to us, and the main one a little farther away. The downtown one was bigger in those days, but later was cut down to a smaller size and other businesses took up their home in the other side. There was a pool hall for awhile, an exercise gym and I don't know what else. Other smaller office type buildings were added on the outside, and included a salon, a dating service, etc.

At this time though, in the early seventies, it was still a bigger Post Office. There was an area around a corner with a larger table for applying postage once you had purchased it, and a place to mail items on your own. I stood in line with my mom as she waited her turn to buy 100 stamps.

When we got up there, she immediately asked the clerk for her desired amount of stamps. The clerk, an older, somewhat brusque, fast-talking guy, inquired of her, "You want a roll or a sheet?"

I turned white. Thought I was going to pass out. Eleven-Year-Old Has Heart Attack in Post Office. This couldn't be! Since when did they have such strict laws? The guy got a strange look on his face, which only confirmed to me that I had heard right.

Later, when we had walked around to the other area so my mom could apply her stamps, I whispered to her, "What did he ask you?"

"He asked if I wanted a roll or a sheet of stamps," she replied.

Ohhh - the realization hit home, and relief set in. For I was sure he had said, "How old is she?" Since when do you have to be over 21 to go into the Post Office? When did these Federal regulations go into effect? What did they think I was going to do – get high off the stamp glue? I was convinced I was going to be thrown out on my ear.

Had I been older, I might have thought he said, "You wanna roll in the sheets?" Good thing I had never heard that phrase back then. In that case, the guy really would have given me a weird look when I collapsed on the floor!

43. Spurting my Juices

Bad timing. I've seen a lot of it. As adults, we may consider these to be the times when we finally decide to buy something we've considered for awhile, and it goes on sale the next day. Or maybe you sell some stock and it goes way up as soon as you're out of the picture. This, however, is not exactly what I'm referring to here. On a kid scale, one of the most common examples of bad timing is when someone makes you laugh right after you've taken a mouthful of something wet. The results can be disastrous, as you will see. Two examples of personal experience come to mind.

Both of these happened in sixth grade, if I remember correctly. One was at the lunch table at school, and the other was at a meeting of Camp Fire Girls.

There was the Camp Fire meeting, held at a different girl's house every week. This may have been fifth grade – I'm not sure. We all had Cokes that day, as we had our after-school snack before beginning our meeting. One of the girls in the group had a male dog, named Tuffy. Another girl had a female dog, named Cindy. They knew each other well – lived on the same street.

The subject of these dogs came up, and one of the girls wanted to say, "Cindy's Tuffy's aunt". Instead, she got confused and said, "Tuffy's Cindy's aunt!"

Ooh, here was the bad timing. Unfortunately, I had taken a good mouthful of Coke, the sticky, sugary stuff, which I shared with everyone at the table. I was generous to a fault. Cleanup time!

Now, this one, for sure, was in sixth grade. Someone had donated some freshly painted and stained picnic tables to our school. Before that, we used to just sit on the blacktop outside of our classrooms to eat our lunches. But these tables, with benches attached, had been painted partly in a nice rich green and partly stained in a medium golden brown with a shiny finish.

It seemed this one day, that someone at our table was talking with her mouth full, and it was annoying one of the other students, a good friend of mine. My friend decided to confront her by telling her not to talk with food in her mouth. Instead, the words that came out of her mouth were, "Talk with your mouth shut!"

Uh, oh…This time, I had just taken either a good slug of milk or a mouthful of soup, whatever I had that day. Everybody ended up getting some, as I snorted back a laugh and sprayed my liquid, possibly even noodles. Gee-rossssss!

Maybe I could have helped her out. I believe what she really meant was, "Don't eat with food in your mouth!"

44. You Can Always Depend on Frank

In seventh grade, a teacher who we only had for a few months before she resigned, (I never did know why), decided to give us a fun way of learning our vocabulary. She divided the class in half; I believe three rows each, to make teams for playing Password.

Before beginning the game, we were all allowed to study a printed list of words for a certain number of minutes. After we had all put away our lists so we couldn't cheat, and had to depend on our memories, she would call one student up from each side to give clues to their team. Each side was only allowed one clue at a time. If the first student called on didn't know the correct answer, it was the next team's turn, no matter how many of the others might have gotten it right. A lot had to do with who was called on. If I remember right, the student who gave the right answer was allowed to replace the former student up front.

The teacher would secretly show the word she wanted done next, to the two people giving clues up front. That's when they would start taking turns throwing out one-word clues to their side, and choosing whose name to call.

Another handicap involved which student the teacher picked to give the clues. If someone didn't have that great a vocabulary to begin with, it could cause a slight problem with them coming up with accurate clues. This happened on my side of the room, when the teacher started with Rod, a kid who was known more for goofing around then being studious. This was the same kid who later tried to pass off the sentence, "I saw the harass" on a spelling test because he didn't know what the word meant, and was too lazy to look it up before the test.

When the teacher showed him the word in the Password game, he immediately said to her, "I don't know what it means!" She told him he could pass, but only once. If the other side didn't get it, and the turn was passed back to his side, he would need to come up with something. Sometimes, just listening to the last clue given could give the other person an idea. But, not so, in the case with Rod.

When the clue was given for the other side, I immediately recognized that the word in question was "rely". I believe the clue was "depend". Lots of hands went up for that side, but the wrong person was picked, and it immediately defaulted to our side. Now, it was up to Rod to carry the ball.

Instead, he turned to the teacher and said, "I still don't know what it means!"

The teacher answered him, "Well, then just say anything."

Rod faced us with a somewhat impish and flippant look, shrugged, and blurted out, "hot dog!"

Immediately, my hand shot up, along with a number of others. Rod pointed at me. I was surprised that he called on me, because he'd always hated me. Maybe he had just enough sense to know that I had a better vocabulary than some of the others and would score a point in his favor.

"Rely!" I replied triumphantly.

Giggles and a tally mark went up for our side, proving that it paid to listen on both sides.

The teacher laughed along with us, whispering, "hot dog!" as I took Rod's place. But she still resigned later, for mysterious reasons. Maybe we just hadn't been frank enough with her.

45. Going Courting

During one of my junior high years, my teacher thought it would be good for us to visit a courthouse to watch a few cases in action. It may have been educational at the time, but I don't remember much about it. For some in the class, it was just another chance to cut up, as they often did in the classroom.

We sat in the back of the courtroom, watching the various cases for the day. All I remember was hearing a guy talk about a "crick" with a bridge running over it. I think he was disputing a traffic ticket, but I don't really remember the details. In those days, I was too busy looking around, possibly dodging fists and flying objects from my classmates, to concentrate on much of anything in my classes. It was a solid two years of chaos in that school.

After the judge was done with his cases, many of the people who had been sitting in the back watching left the courthouse. Our class alone remained. The judge announced that he had been told there was a class of seventh-graders visiting, and opened the floor for questions. Hands flew from various students, and one by one they stood up to state their inquiries. One girl repeatedly addressed the judge as "Your Honor", the only one who did, I believe. Some of the others made fun of her, snickered at her, but it didn't curb her obvious show of respect. She was probably the only one who remembered the answers to the questions, too. The others may well have been just trying to sound important and intelligent by asking whatever came to them. She seemed to truly want to learn, and she got my respect by showing her own.

At some point, one of the boys asked if he could come up and sit at the judge's bench. He was given permission. I don't know if he was the only one, or if some took turns, but I think the judge left the room after that, asking that we leave things as we found them. I know this kid sat up there for awhile.

All of a sudden, a middle-aged man burst into the room, asking frantically, "did somebody in here push a button?"

If anybody did, they wouldn't admit to it. Or maybe I should say, they didn't "cop" to it. For, under certain pieces of furniture in the courtroom, or maybe just under the judge's bench, a button was hidden that would summon officers from the nearby police station. This was an emergency precaution that could be set off silently if things got "too hairy" in the courtroom during a difficult case.

The man explained this to us, and stood there for awhile, panting and trying to compose himself. "I'm too old to run!" he finally declared breathlessly.

Stuart, the kid up front, who was a well-known troublemaker in our school, found this hilarious. Letting out a giggle and a sadistic chuckle, he yelled dramatically, "I'm too young to die!"

The older man didn't see the humorous side of Stuart's remark. After finally slowing down his breathing, he left us with warnings to be careful not to push anything else. It was back to the police station for him, to wait for the next bit of excitement.

It's a wonder we got out of there without somebody being arrested. We left shortly after, with the newfound knowledge of this concealed button, if nothing else.

Maybe they should have arrested Stuart. Then we'd have another case to watch. Most likely, though, it would have been scheduled for another day. Probably on a Saturday, when we'd rather stay home, even if it would mean seeing that creepy kid get in trouble.

46. Fighting Fire with Fire Before the Fire

Back around 1972 or 1973, I was looking out the living room window one evening when I noticed a commotion on the sidewalk. It seemed that this took place in the summer, but it may have just been at a time when the weather was friendly toward kids who wanted to play outside after dinner. What I saw was the kid next door, about 7 years old at the time, tormenting a girl who seemed to be younger. I have no idea who she was, since all I could see was the backside of her, running like the wind, away from this kid and some of his friends. And what she was running from were the taunts of these boys, yelling such things as:

"I'm the Red Devil!"

"I'm the Bloody Finger!"

"I use pink toilet paper!"

All of these remarks followed by heavy giggles and snorts.

I'd run too. Especially knowing these kids and the rest of the family connected with this one next door. We'd had a number of run-ins with them since moving into the neighborhood in 1966. They were originals, just like us – the first owners of these new houses built in place of the cherry and apricot orchards.

I believe this kid's mother came out around that time and stopped them. But it was one of the few times she'd done so. Usually this family's kids got away with a lot, and their parents defended them to other parents whose kids would often retaliate. The older kids in the neighborhood were usually reminded by this lady that her kid was younger, even though he did weigh 60 pounds when he was two years old, and was strong and mean from the beginning.

A day or so after this incident, my mom went out to get the newspaper in the morning and found a note on our front step. Written in pencil in ghastly-looking shaky printing were the words, "Red Devil strikes again!"

My mom showed it to me, mocking terror as she wondered where it came from. I told her what I had witnessed, and gave her my guess as to who had written it.

A couple of evenings later, the doorbell rang. My mom went to open it, only to find nobody there. This was a case of doorbell ditch, which is what makes me think it happened in the summer. Though there was nobody to be seen, another note was lying there, similar to the last one. This one was written in black felt pen, included a picture of a cloud with lightning coming out of it, and read, "Black Lightning strikes again!"

My mom decided not to let this keep up much longer. One evening she wrote a somewhat ominous note that read:

If the Red Devil or Black Lightning return, the Terrible Powers that Be will descend upon them

I believe this referred to our last name. I'm not the only one in the family who can come up with bad puns. She taped the sign up on the door, turned off the light and sat in a chair in the living room waiting for them to come back. They never did. I think she was a bit disappointed; she'd planned to sneak to the front door and open it, just as they went to ring the bell. She never did get to confront them.

Sometime later, on March 1st of 1973, which I believe was a Thursday, I was getting ready to be driven to school when the doorbell rang early in the morning. My mom went to answer it and found nobody there. Immediately remembering the antics of the kid next door, she yelled, "All right, you guys, I've had..." and stopped when she saw an unfamiliar man standing in our grass.

"There's a house on fire!" the guy informed us.

"Where?" my mom asked.

"Next door."

We immediately got out in case it spread to our house, forgetting that my sister was still in bed upstairs. After we were safely outside, I voiced the fear that my dog would get burned up. Since the fire hadn't spread in our direction, we went inside, quickly got a leash from the closet, and hooked up the dog to save her. That's when my sister came down in her robe, indignant that we'd left her up there. It turned out that when the guy had said, "next door", she'd thought he said "back door". She was sure it was our house that was on fire, and we had left her to burn, coming back only for the dog.

Their house was pretty well destroyed, and most of the animals with it. There was a puppy that had been born in that house, the mother dog having been destroyed some time earlier after she had attacked my dog for the second time, almost killing her. The puppy happened to be in the garage, which didn't get burned. Someone opened the garage door, and she came running out, happily wagging at being saved. One of the cats was already outside when the fire started, and lived. We saw him on the fence a day or two after, and knew he'd escaped. But another cat, 14 years old, and with them since the oldest kid in the family was a baby, was inside and didn't make it out. He was too feeble, and wasn't used to going out much anymore.

The youngest kid, about seven or eight at the time, (the Red Devil) was seen on the sidewalk at some point, talking to one of the firemen about his pet mice and hamsters. Unfortunately, they weren't saved either.

But all of the people made it out. The mother had been driving back home from a nearby city, and had seen smoke in her area. Knowing that it was somewhere in her neighborhood, she had no idea that it was her house. The youngest kid had just been getting ready to leave for school when it started. The two older kids were either already headed for school, or were around somewhere in the crowd on the street.

They believe the fire was started by a pan of grease on the stove. The lady had been frying doughnuts the night before, and the pan had been left sitting there. Someone must have turned it on accidentally, or it was left on low for awhile. Whatever the case, the entire house had to be rebuilt, which took several months. During the rainy season, the whole neighborhood had a smoky smell from the charred remains. Bits of blackened stucco from the walls remained in our backyard for a long time. Two carved light-brown wooden cats, which I remembered being in their front hall were thrown outside in front, completely black, full of ash and cracked.

After the house was rebuilt and they had moved back in, things got a little easier with them for awhile. They seemed truly grateful for all the help they got from the neighbors, such as meals and desserts. At one point, they mentioned the plan to throw a block party for everyone to show their appreciation for the treatment they had received. But it never happened. Sometime after, they went back to their normal selves, the lady refusing to talk to us or even acknowledge us in public after one of the spats between her kids and us. Once she almost ran into a bank of gum machines in a grocery store because she was trying so hard to avoid us. Later, when they sent their kid to a Christian school, he was nicer to us, and sometimes looked as if he wanted to talk to us, but seemed uncomfortable as if he'd been instructed not to. But the parents didn't change; they didn't have to. They weren't the ones being taught in the Christian school.

Much later, they moved to a distant state, and I haven't seen or heard of any of them since. Over the years, the

159

neighborhood has turned over a lot, with older families moving out or dying, and new ones with kids coming in. At this point, however, the Red Devil and Black Lightning have not returned. But the Terrible Powers' are still there waiting for them.

47. Seeing Stars at the Movies

Some time back in the '70s, a new shopping center was built in the adjoining town, about 5 miles from where we lived. We didn't go there often; most of the stores were too expensive, and the one I always wanted to check out, my mom warned me that the salesmen were too pushy and would follow you around the place even after you told them you were just looking. So I always had to look inside from afar, and was never able to go in. I think by the time I was driving, the shopping center had closed down, so it was too late for me to check it out on my own.

One thing we did do there, though, was go to the movie theatre. Sometimes a movie we wanted to see would only be playing there, or the times were more convenient for us than at other theatres.

One evening, or early afternoon, my mom, my sister and I headed over there for a movie that was listed. My mom was driving, my sister riding in front and me in the back seat.

Either that was a really popular movie, or there was something else going on there at the time. Finding a parking space was close to impossible as we drove around and around repeatedly.

Finally, after taking a vast tour, and practically memorizing the cars and all their license plates, we spotted an open space a row or two over. My mom instantly headed there. And as we neared the area, we observed another car pulling into our desired slot. My mom let out an exclamation as the other car neatly pulled in.

We then passed by the formerly empty spot, just as the driver and her passenger were getting out and locking up. That's when my mom, in mild surprise, stated, "that's Joan Baez!"

"So it is!" my sister mused.

I must have been kicking back with my eyes closed, or possibly half lying down resting until we could park. I looked out, just in time to see this lady, who was probably used to being recognized in public, turning and flashing a big smile at us.

"She took my parking space!" my mom fumed lightly.

And my sister noticed something else. "Her kid is taller than I am!"

My sister's short stature had always been a source of chagrin to her. My brother, two years younger than she, suddenly shot up taller when he was about 11 or 12. He found it highly amusing to look down at her and say, "What 'cha doin' down there, Shorty?"…or rest his elbow on her shoulder like she was a piece of furniture. He teased her relentlessly, but she continued to refer to him as her "little brother" when talking on the phone with her friends. Once when I was about 8 or 9, I told her she should answer him with, "I don't like your altitude!" Years later, when my brother had his own daughter, he would often ask her if she was taller than my sister yet. We didn't see them often, so when they would come one to three times a year, my brother had to rub in the fact that his kid was already coming up close on my sister when she was about 12, and my sister about 38. And his daughter did finally pass up my sister. My brother has never let up on this, as far as I know. Maybe he'll start it with his two-year-old and baby granddaughters soon.

But here we were in the car in a shopping center, seeing this kid who had been featured in a baby picture in one of his mother's record albums, and he was already taller than my sister! I'm not sure he was even a teenager yet himself, but he was close.

The rest of the time, as we drove around the parking lot looking for another space, there was a constant repeated litany of "Joan Baez took my parking space!" from my mom, interspersed with, "her kid is taller than I am!" from my sister. Two voices, two grievances. I think it was more entertaining for me than the movie we were about to see.

Then, my mom spotted another empty space in the next row and made a beeline for it. As we got closer, I exclaimed in mock horror, "Uh, oh, looks like Peter, Paul and Mary got that one!"

My mom was not amused, but my sister was, and snickered. She commented that it would be funny if there had been three separate spaces and Peter, Paul and Mary each had their own car. We both broke up, with my mom threatening not to pay for our movie tickets if we didn't behave. My sister threw me a look – a grimace of pretend fear.

As it turned out, the space was still open when we got over there. I had been joshing her. We got out of the car, locked up and went to stand in line. My mom gave the money to my sister to buy tickets for all of us, saying she needed to find a bathroom first.

As soon as she was out of earshot, my sister turned to me.

"*Peter, Paul and Mary,* you wiseass!" she admonished me with a grin. We practically rolled on the concrete outside the theatre.

I don't even remember what the movie was. Probably something I hated; there wasn't much in the '70s that I remember wanting to see again. But there are still times when my mom will reminisce in mock grimness on the day we had our parking place confiscated by Joan Baez.

And her kid is probably a *lot* taller than my sister is by now!

48. Waxing Poetic

This is a story I heard from the family involved, many years after it happened. I don't know if I have all of the details correct, and half of that family is deceased at this time, so checking it would be difficult, but not impossible. One daughter is fairly nearby, but I think I have the main story, so I believe it's unnecessary to contact her.

At some time, early in the formation of this family, the parents acquired a fairly expensive, exquisitely detailed molded wax Nativity set. I don't remember if it was a whole set (doubtful), just the Holy Family or just the Christ Child. In any case, it was well-made, possibly hand-molded or maybe cast in a mold, and I think, from Italy, or some faraway land such as this.

This was set up for display somewhere in their house during the Christmas season. One day, one of the parents walked by and noticed an arm or leg missing from their baby lying in the manger.

Shortly after this, the older daughter, probably 4 or 5 at the time came to her mother and confided, "Mary ate Baby Jesus!"

Mind you, she wasn't referring to the Mother of God in this incident. Mary was her baby sister, probably about a year old, or at least less than 2 years old.

Some time later, another limb was missing from the figure. Again, the older daughter tipped off her parents with the words, "Mary ate Baby Jesus!"

I don't know how long it was before the parents found out the truth. Maybe they caught the older girl in the act of munching. But the cold, hard fact of the matter was that the older sister was the one who had, "eaten Baby Jesus". Mary, too young to talk and defend herself at the time, had become the innocent victim of her sister's desire to chew on some wax.

Mary, as it turned out, was destined to a hard, short and pain-filled life. Found to have a serious kidney disease at an early age, she had her first transplant when she was around 13 or 14. Later, she received another one when she was about 36, as a result of a fatal accident suffered by a generous donor. And finally, at the age of 40, she was on a waiting list for another one when she became pregnant. Having the baby did her in; the baby was born healthy, but Mary slipped into a coma. It literally took everything out of her, and she died shortly after.

The parents of this family are the other deceased members, so they probably already know about their daughter's demise. But when the older daughter gets there, I've often wondered if her first words to her parents will be, "Mary met Baby Jesus!"

49. Always Acknowledge Cat Trophies Immediately!

This one is more of a "Kitty Perception" but exhibits some of the same traits as a "Kiddie Perception". Cats can sometimes have the same characteristics as little kids.

My cat had been forced to move back to my parents' house while I was in my second apartment. She stayed there for the rest of her life, even though I was in a different apartment for awhile in between my own stays at my parents' house.

One day I came home and found my cat sitting up on the roof waiting for me. I had always been amazed at how animals could distinguish the sound of their owners' cars over all others in the area. When my brother had two of his dogs living in my parents' backyard, they would often start barking in the evening when he was on the way home. Sometimes it would be twenty minutes before he showed up, but sure enough, the dogs were right. It had been his car on the way.

My cat would often be on the front step, on the driveway, on the roof or heading down the fence as I drove up. I expected this, and wasn't surprised when she was up on the roof watching for me that day.

What did surprise me was that as soon as I got out of the car, she ran quickly toward the back of the house instead of coming down by the gate on the side to greet me. I couldn't figure out what had attracted her attention.

I headed over toward the side of the house and called her name. She came almost right away, but she wasn't alone. Dangling from her mouth was her latest prize trophy – a very large scraggly dead mouse.

Did I immediately praise her great hunting skills? Well, no, not unless you count, "Oh, gross, Raisin, get that thing outta here!" as praise.

Instead of obeying, she tried numerous times throughout that day to get me to respond properly. I wasn't learning quickly enough.

Shortly after I came inside, I headed for a downstairs room that originally was the domain of my oldest brother. This room had been turned into a craft room, and has also been used for a lot of storage during quick clean-ups. It usually has to be weeded through several times a year to prevent someone getting lost in there. At this time, however, it had just been straightened out so I could spend some time in there making my dollhouse miniatures I sold to stores.

My cat, unfortunately, still had good hearing for things besides distinguishing car motors. She knew what room I was in. After I had sat down at the long table under the window, she came to the edge of the roof, skillfully leaned out and dangled her rodent at me.

"Raisin, get outta here with that!" I screamed at her again. I got up immediately and closed the curtain.

She must have thought I did that to get the sun out of my eyes. That was part of it, but not the main part. A few minutes later, I heard her meowing outside that same window. I let her keep it up for awhile, but then thought about it. Could she possibly form the word "meow" with a mouthful of mouse? I didn't think so – the 'm' would be muffled. Maybe she had put it down and just wanted to talk to me.

I opened the curtain partway. And there she was, sitting up there again with this ragged looking thing hanging disgustingly from her lips. It was starting to get really shaggy and used looking. Maybe she had put it down while she called to me, and just picked it up when she heard me coming. Or maybe cats don't form words with their lips like people do. Or maybe I had a talented ventriloquist of a cat and just didn't know it. I yelled at her again, closing the curtain.

Shortly after, I realized it was lunchtime. I headed for the refrigerator, gleefully finding a bockwurst in there. I had been crazy about these for years. One problem here, though. These sausages were grey, the same color as my cat's latest trophy.

I made my sandwich and took it to the table, trying to forget about my furry feline friend, Raisin's prize. Too late, I realized, the sliding glass door in the family room was right across from the large passageway between the kitchen table and family room. My cat figured this out before I did, and was sitting at the door watching me try to eat something grey as she once again attempted to show me what a good mouser she was. I'll show you my grey thing if you'll show me yours! Ugh! I closed that curtain too, and yelled at her again.

She either finally got the message or gave up, accepting my retching noises as praise. If I'd known better, I would have closed my eyes and praised her the first time. Maybe she would have gone off and found something else to do, even if it was to hunt something else. Instead, me being a slow learner on stuff like this, and not having gotten advice from another cat owner until later, I had to endure this over and over that day. I don't have a cat now, so I can't try the other approach yet. Maybe someday, but I think the next one is going to be kept indoors!

50. Picture This!

When my brother's daughter was about 3, sometime in the early 1980's, she stayed at my parents' house for a week. Grandma thought it would be fun to have her there, on her own trip without her parents. I think her parents had been there for a weekend, and the plan was to leave her at Grandma & Grandpa's house for a week, and have them drive her home the next weekend. It was a 3 or 4 hour drive, so it was a big deal for her.

I don't think I was living at home at that time, but I was only about 20 minutes away. I managed to somehow come over every day. Any reason seemed to be good enough. One morning my mom called me and said the kid had something to tell me. She got on the phone and informed me, "You need to come over and blow bubbles outside!"

I told her, "I knew there was something I needed to do!"

Seems she had tried to get Grandma to blow bubbles, and Grandma didn't want to do it, and wouldn't let her do it in the house. So she pawned the kid off on me. Sneaky Grandma!

I had recently been laid off from my first, and longest running job, and hadn't been able to find anything else. It might have had something to do with the fact that everybody else was laying off also. So I was available a lot during the days.

One day, during this week, my mom told my sister she had an idea. Sometime before the kid went home, my sister and I should dress her up fancy, take her to the mall and have her picture taken professionally. Notice my mom came up with the ideas, but suggested that someone else implement them!

The mall downtown had a Kinderfoto, one of the more popular kiddie studios around at the time. My mom would pay to have this done if we'd take her.

So we did. Only things didn't work out exactly as we expected. We ended up spending most of the day in the mall, and mostly in this studio.

I don't think she liked the first photographer much. And I understood why. She had a certain personality that I had run up against before. It's hard to explain; sort of an attitude of phoniness in dealing with kids at the same time that she thought she was real good at it. Almost like the social awkwardness of a teenager. This photographer reminded me of when I was 5, and one of my cousins, who was about 7, would walk over to me and pick me up. Drove me stark raving nuts. She could barely heft me, and I could tell she wasn't strong enough to hold me up long. Also, it was sheer humiliation to have a kid pick me up at that age. There wasn't that much difference in our ages, and she was treating me like a baby.

That wasn't exactly what the photographer was doing, but there was a certain expression in her face that showed she couldn't handle kids as well as she may have thought. And I think the kid sensed it, as they often do.

These photographers do have tricks to get kids to laugh or smile. Hers was to hold up a very flimsy collapsible cardboard box, open it up and look through the open ends, calling the kid's name and then flatten it and wave it in her face to blow air at her. Apparently this had worked with some kids. Not this one, though.

She tried it a number of times, only to be met with a stony face. After awhile, it got close to lunchtime, so the photographer suggested we go out on the mall, shop around, maybe have lunch and come back later to try again.

As it turned out, we did this several times. Each time we came back, the kid made it clear that she wasn't going to smile, or even pretend to. So we'd go off in the mall for awhile again.

At that time, the concept of craft malls was fairly new. There was a certain one that had a location in another shopping center, and they had recently opened another in this center. These were places where crafters and artists could rent a booth, display their wares, and let the store sell them without the artist having to be there all the time. They may have required the artist to work in the store for a certain number of hours during each month. I know that's how a lot of the more recently established ones work.

We decided to stop in this location and look at the wares. There were wooden carved items, stained glass sun catchers, jewelry, pottery, etc. When we got to the stained glass, we found the sun catchers to be of the variety that had been strung with fishing line or clear nylon thread so they would dangle without seeming to be held up by anything. My niece immediately started batting at them, spinning them with her hand and saying gleefully, "it goes 'round and 'round!" My sister and I both cringed, thinking we were about to pay for this artist's entire supply of ruined wares. We diverted her, and quickly left that store.

Once more, back at the studio, the photographer tried again with no results.

Finally, out of ideas, and somewhat exhausted she looked to us, the wise and knowing aunts. "How do you get her to laugh at home?" she asked wearily.

My sister gestured toward me, grimacing. "Terri makes weird obnoxious noises!" she confessed.

The photographer gave me beseeching eyes. "Would you...?"

Oh, man!! Right here on the mall? There were people walking by! I complied grudgingly.

Once inside the store, I planted myself squarely in front of the kid.

"Meow, meow, meow!" I said, in mock harshness, as I usually did with her. "Hyee, hyee, hyeeeuhhh!" I grimaced fiercely. This normally produced heavy giggles.

The kid stared at me like I was a stranger, her face deadpan.

I tried again. "HYEEEE, Hyee, **hyee**, hyeeeuhhh!" with emphasis this time."MEOW, MYA, MEOW!!!!"

Again, no sign of recognition on her part. And the strangers filtering past in the mall were treated to my performance. The things I'll do!

Lucky for all of us, this photographer was about to either end her shift or go to lunch herself. Another photographer, this one a little more jolly and open showed up to take over. She was informed of the techniques that had already been used, and said she'd try something different.

She also held up the collapsible box, but instead of just calling through it, she rolled a small rubber ball through it and caught it on the other end. These people were trained to move smoothly, catching, collapsing the box, waving it to create breeze, and aiming & clicking the camera at just the right time.

And this time, the kid liked it! I don't know if it was just the difference of the rubber ball, small and red like the ones used in jacks, or if she just liked this person better. But she laughed, smiled, held the fake flower in one shot, a lacy parasol in another, posing in front of different scenes and did exactly what we had hoped to accomplish from the start. We were out of there in a hurry.

Somehow, she didn't trust us to leave the mall that time. She had been brought back and forth too many times, and seemed to think we'd be doing it again. We had done some shopping; it may have been that same trip when my sister had bought her some fancy hair ribbons, but the kid seemed to think we weren't done after we finally got the pictures taken. As we walked, and partially ran through the mall toward the main doors, the kid kept sobbing, "Ride car-car!" meaning she wanted to leave. My sister kept trying to reassure her, but she wasn't buying it. We'd made her think this was happening too many times already. Until she was in the car, we weren't going to convince her we were going back to Grandma's.

The pictures turned out great; you never would have known there was any problem, except those who were waiting at home wondered what took us so long. Later, when my oldest brother heard about my antics and circus act "Meowing at the Mall", he said, "She was probably too embarrassed to laugh! She was probably saying, 'not here, Terri!'" It wasn't my idea anyway; it was an act of desperation.

I wonder why my mom never suggested this type of expedition with my nephew 13 years later. He was the one who did an imitation of a cat meowing and acting out the "hokey-pokey" on all fours when he was about the same age my niece had been. He probably would have enjoyed my performance. Besides, he always smiled and flirted with strangers on the street anyway.

I think maybe that studio was gone from the mall by then. Most likely, they'd had all of their photographers quit in frustration.

51. Don't Put Flatware in the Washing Machine

This is not exactly a "Kiddie Perception" – I was in my mid-20s when it happened, but it was such a strange experience, it may as well have been.

I hated doing dishes by hand, flat-out couldn't stand it, never could. Especially in this studio apartment I had at the time, which contained no dishwasher. The first two apartments I lived in had dishwashers, and even then I would wait a few days sometimes before loading it.

In this, my third apartment, though, there was no dishwasher. Everything had to be done by hand. It was one of those tiny kitchens, where you would turn one way to be at the sink, and another to be at the counter. The refrigerator was crammed in a corner by the wall, and would often open with a bang, hitting the wall as it barely cleared the stove on the other side.

Somehow, it never hit me that it would be easier to do small amounts of dishes each time instead of letting it build up over a few weeks. Only when I would come inside and realize that my apartment smelled worse than the cruddy air outside, did I consider washing some of my stuff. Also, that was usually about the same time I ran out of clean stuff to use. It was either starve or wash, although in those days, I lived right in the hub of junk food city. I discovered right after I moved into that place that I was within either walking or close-driving distance of a McDonald's, Dairy Queen, two 7-11 stores, a Taco Bell, A&W, KFC, H. Salt's Fish & Chips, Baskin Robbins, Carl's Jr., Pioneer Chicken and Der Weinerschnitzel. I found the Burger King much later, a little farther away in another direction. Only when I was moving out did they build a Burger King real close to the place where I lived, on a lot which used to house a business called "TV Doctor". It took me awhile to figure out what used to be there. They'd had a white sign with a red cross on it and the name of the TV repair shop. The Burger King didn't last long there, though. Like I said, I was moving out at the time. They missed out on having a regular customer, though the Dairy Queen had often been filled at lunchtime by the nurses from the hospital across the street and Postal Carriers on their lunch break. It seemed that the Burger King would have been able to make a go of it, but for some reason, a couple years later when I went back to the area, they had another Taco Bell in there.

Not that they had gotten rid of the one at the other end of the street. They left that there, but it was one of the older small versions with few tables, and this was one of the bigger ones with indoor seating besides the tiny tables attached to the outside of the building. We had our choice of being squashed into the small outdoor chairs or overcrowded by screaming kids running around unchecked inside. Strangely enough, the Dairy Queen was also gone, having been torn down and replaced with a much larger parking lot for the 7-11 crowd.

I did go to some of these places in the 5 years I lived there, but I also tried to save some money by doing some real cooking at home. That's when the flatware and dishes would pile up. I had to do something, but I really dreaded it sometimes.

Sometimes, my laziness would be in full throttle, and I would only wash as much as I needed for a few days, leaving the rest of the stinky mess in the sink to grow more interesting stuff on it. Other times I would give up and plunge into the whole thing, hating every second, but watching the pile go down.

One day, the idea hit me to gather it all up, take it down to the laundry room and run it through the washing machine. Slothfulness will inspire you that way sometimes.

I didn't do it right away, but mentioned it to my mom the next time I went home. She warned me not to, saying it might cause chips in the enamel finish, resulting in rust bleeding on mine or someone else's clothes later.

I waited a few more days, and finally decided to try it anyway. If it didn't work well the first time, or caused problems, I wouldn't do it again. Who, me, disobey my mother? Well, yeah.

I think it might have been early in the morning, during the time that the laundry room was locked and we weren't supposed to be in there. I had found long ago, that the key to the bottom lock on all of the apartment doors opened the laundry room, and also the "security doors" at the ends of the hallway. I put "security" in quotes, because most of the time during the summer, the doors were wide open at each end to get some breeze in there. This was especially true on the top floor where I lived; in the winter I'd turn off my heater and just collect heat from the two floors below me, resulting in a heating bill of $5 to $30. In the summer, however, we'd collect the stifling heat from all over. I noticed when I would walk up the steps in the stairwell that the heat would just hang in an invisible cloud that would assault people when they'd reach the top floor. The management didn't see fit to put fans in the hallways, so we had to prop the doors open. I noticed one day that one apartment had an air conditioner sticking out the window. It turned out to be the assistant manager's place. She may have installed it herself.

On the morning of my planned crime, I gathered all of my silverware in a paper bag and headed to the first floor. I let myself into the laundry room with my key, selected a washer and started pulling handfuls of silverware from the bag, trying not to make too much noise. I laid them gently inside the machine, added soap and set the cycle. After hearing it start, I left quickly, getting on the elevator to wait out my time upstairs. I knew that if anyone found out, I had to be prepared to disown my entire set of flatware and buy more somewhere, rather than cop to it. I had plans.

Sometime later, I came down to retrieve it with a paper bag folded neatly. I got off the elevator just in time to see one of the maintenance guys coming out of the laundry room, shaking his head.

"Nothing in here," I heard him mutter. I quickly tucked my brown bag under my arm and ducked down the hallway, pretending to head out to my car in the parking lot. After I heard the side door close, and was pretty sure he was heading back to the office to call the tenant who had reported noise, I came back, quickly loaded my stuff into the bag, and rolled it up. The bag was getting pretty wet and starting to tear. I made a point of rolling it up tightly so there would be extra layers of paper, preventing my entire set of silverware from clattering against the tile floor in the lobby. I worked fast, tucking it under my arm and hopping on the elevator.

By the time I got to the top floor, I was seeing large rips in the paper. I got inside just in time and dumped everything on the counter.

Besides this stuff being noisy as it clattered through the wash and rinse cycles, it didn't really get very clean. It may have had hot enough water to sterilize the items, but there were giant spots on them. I still had to re-rinse each piece, but I didn't have to scrub as hard as I might have if I'd done it all in the sink.

Still, it was a close call. I had been prepared to abandon everything if I saw a maintenance guy or manager discovering what I'd done. But I wasn't crazy about the possibility of having to shell out money for new stuff.

Sometime later, I was on the phone with a guy I had gone to school with years before. I told him how much I hated doing dishes by hand, and he told me of a trick he had played on a former roommate who didn't hold up his end of turn-taking with dishes. It seemed that one evening, he collected up a bunch of dishes that had been left all over the apartment and piled them in a large stack in the sink to get this guy's attention. I don't remember if he said he ended up breaking a bunch of plates in the sink, or just piling them high so his friend would get the message.

One of his next sentences to me had a profound effect on me, at least for awhile. He said something like, "What's such a drag about being able to put your hands in hot soapy water and moving around in it?" He made it sound like a bubble bath. For weeks after that, I did my dishes almost every day. The effect wore off after awhile, but I considered calling him again and making him repeat that. I didn't though, just called upon my memory and got jump-started again. It is something worth remembering.

52. Pizza Junk

Okay, this isn't a Kiddie Perception either, but it certainly could have been, just like the last one. I have never seen anything like it, before or since. A fine example of things being not as they seem.

In 1986, I was working at a Post Office in a tourist town about 30 minutes away from where I lived at the time. It was mainly a minimum wage town; if you didn't have a government job, you were pretty much resigned to selling ice cream, hamburgers and the like, or running a motel or inn for the many tourists who either came through, or would rent a room for a couple of weeks to a month.

This was an area known mostly for its beaches and gift shops, rife with tourists and leftover hippies who couldn't give up what had clearly become passé. I had tried to get into a Post Office closer to home, but in order to hone my test taking skills, I had signed up to take the Postal exam in different areas. Each time, even though the tests were slightly different, my score would go up. I ended up getting a 99.5 in this city. It still took me a year or two to get hired there.

In the years prior to this, I had become known for making a whole-wheat pizza crust, as I had been taken off white flour several times by various doctors. After working in this Post Office for a short time, I discovered a place across the street in this downtown area whose sign boasted pizza with whole-wheat crust. I had to try it.

Only problem was, they didn't open until 11:00 a.m. I quickly learned that when you're a clerk sorting mail in the back room of the P.O., they usually have you come in very early in the morning, so you can have it sorted by Carrier Route by the time the carriers come in around 8:00 a.m. In my case, I was usually brought in at either 3:05 or 3:35 a.m. And since they didn't want the new people to get any more overtime than necessary, I was often sent home by about 9:00 or 10:00 a.m., usually right after the P.O. Box mail had been sorted. They also gave me a lunch break in there; I never was quite sure what to do with it, since it was nowhere near lunchtime.

We were not allowed to park in the P.O. parking lot – only Postal vehicles could be in there and maybe the supervisor's car. Since there was construction being done on the two-level free parking lot behind our office, there were often times when one or both levels would be taped off and signs posted to keep cars out. On the days when both levels were off-limits, we had to find parking on the street. And since that kind of city often has parking meters, we had to look partway up the road for a space in the area that didn't. I would end up walking in the early morning hours in the dark, freaked out over who might be lurking in the bushes.

Once, when some of us got there early, before our supervisor showed up to unlock the place, we saw a guy sleeping on the loading dock with his feet sticking out onto some of the side steps. I had noticed the feet the first time I walked by, and quickly went back toward my car. When I came back later, I heard one of the other clerks scream, and another clerk showed up to tell the guy he had to go somewhere else. Since I hadn't seen anything but feet, I didn't know if he was just crashing there, or crouching in wait for someone. That's why I made sure I didn't go back until it was closer to the time for others to be there. Most of them lived in the area, and didn't leave home as early as I did.

At some point, after I had worked there a couple of months, I developed a heavy cough, something that used to happen every year until I discovered I was diabetic. It did seem to happen more often if I ate sugar, but I also had it come up in mountain areas like this where there were a lot of allergens in the air. I noticed it cleared up a lot when

I would go home, and get worse when I was driving there each day. Still, my supervisor was somehow convinced at first that it had something to do with the night air. So he switched me to a different shift. That didn't last, though. On that shift, I had to do a different job, which required me to stand a lot more. I didn't know that a knee injury I had received in 1985 was still hanging out below the surface, and would nag me "just like new" if I stood too much. I had to request to be put back on early mornings, where I could sit and sort mail. In another, stricter area, I might have been forced to resign, but since these guys were a lot looser than usual, they let me come back to the morning shift and sit at the sorting case.

Still, during the times when I was on a later day shift, from about 11:00 to 5:00, it would cross my mind that I should stop at that pizza place some day before going home. Every day, I would tell myself I would go there for dinner when I got off that evening. And every day, I would walk past the place, decide I was too tired, and wanted to get that nasty curvy mountain road behind me, and get home.

Finally, when I had a day off once, I mentioned the place to my sister, and asked if she would drive down there so we could try the pizza. We probably spent some time at the beach too – I can't imagine her going to that area and skipping the beach. But we eventually ended up at the destination I had eyed for so long... and discovered, early on, that it was a big mistake.

We placed our order and sat down, quickly noticing what a filthy health hazard the place was. It was dark and creepy, besides being unkempt. I was looking for a refill on my water and I asked the guy behind the counter if I could get one. He pointed to a Rubbermaid pitcher on the counter, which didn't look too clean itself and had clearly been filled at their nearest faucet. Maybe even at the outside hose. No

Calistoga, Alhambra or Crystal Geyser for them! And it certainly was not a place with good clean pipes.

My sister mentioned having to go to the bathroom. I suggested that there might be one down the hall. She stated emphatically that she wouldn't dare go to the bathroom in this place; she'd be afraid of what she might catch.

Meanwhile, we sat for the longest time waiting for the pizza, and listening to the endless droning of Indian sitar music playing from God knows where. After awhile, another employee arrived, apologizing for being a little late, and adding, "I don't feel too well. I threw up earlier!"

My sister cringed and gave me an incredulous look. "I'm glad we ordered already!" she mumbled.

A guy who I had often seen sweeping the sidewalk outside the establishment, came in while we were there. As usual, he was wearing what looked like a monk's robe made of grey sweatshirt material. Going behind the counter, he helped himself to a small salad, which he carried to a booth in the corner. After getting settled, he pulled out a small glass jar and proceeded to dump about ¼ to ½ cup of Metamucil on his salad. Go, friar, go!

The pizza finally arrived, and was for the most part inedible. There was too much sauce, not enough spice, and very little flavor. I wasn't sure what the crust was made of - wet cardboard? Play-Doh? Gutter scrapings after a big rain? We left most of it.

Later, we speculated on how this place managed to stay open. Maybe it wasn't really there for the pizza. Could it have been a front for a drug dealer or a house of ill repute? It was hard to tell. We only knew we had wasted our money.

Some years later, when I was no longer working at that Post Office, my sister moved to that city. The pizza place was still there, but nobody I knew went there. My sister had received a local phone book when she moved there, and I spent some time looking through it to see who and what might still be around. I discovered a fairly large ad under "Pizza" for this place. It seemed to still be thriving if they could afford to place an ad like that.

Then I noticed something in the ad that baffled me. These guys catered weddings! I wonder how long those marriages lasted! I couldn't begin to imagine tolerating a reception like that, or the comments that followed from the guests.

And then, three years after I had worked there, a major earthquake hit, doing a lot of damage to that area. When I went back later, after some stores had been rebuilt, I noticed those guys were gone. I wonder why. Maybe the gas from their food caused the tremor in the first place.

53. Bookworms and Crawly Things Always Catch Up

Sometime in 1963 or 1964, possibly parts of both years, a new daily program was introduced in the Kansas City newspaper on teaching your kids how to read at home. This was just before I started kindergarten, and my mom thought this might be a way to get me to start talking to others. This was, after all, during the time that I wasn't talking to many of my neighbors or any adults outside of my family. She checked with some of the parents of other kids who would be in my kindergarten class, and found that they weren't using this program with their kids. Therefore, she thought that if I started school and was the only one who could already read, they wouldn't be able to shut me up. I would be popping up with all of the answers and be cured. It didn't work; I did learn to read, still didn't talk for awhile, but it was worth a try.

Every day, a new letter would be covered on the Comics page. There would be pictures and words starting with the Letter of the Day, and sometimes little tips for an adult to read to the kid to explain ways of remembering what the letter sounded like.

The program didn't stop with the 26 letters. After the basic sounds had been learned, the daily strip would start on vowels as a group, letter combinations, etc. It went on for a long time. And every day, I would cut it out of the newspaper and paste it in a photo album. I still have it.

Several years ago, when my nephew was about 3, I decided to bring the book along while I was babysitting one night. I didn't let on to my sister that I was doing this. I tried to get the kid to keep it a secret, and blow my sister's mind when he could start reading sentences. He agreed, but let it slip partway the next morning when his dad asked what he had done with me the night before. His dad didn't know what he was talking about, and the kid caught himself and wouldn't say anymore, but my sister figured it out. I was met with a sly look from her when I came to do some cleaning at her house the next morning.

He had already learned some of the letter sounds at pre-school, but I had given him a jump. He liked my book enough to ask me to bring it back another time and work with him some more. Even now, at age 11, he remembers that I taught him the sounds of "a" and "e".

At the bottom of the "A" page was a tiny picture of a girl eating an apple with a big green worm coming out of the bitten part of the fruit. It said something like, "If you were eating an apple and a worm crawled out, you might say, 'aaa' just as this girl is saying." It was supposed to help you remember the sound of the letter "a" by thinking of both the "aaa" and the apple. I read this to him, this 3-year-old who liked to garden with his mom. His answer was, "If I was eating an apple and a worm crawled out, I'd say, 'Hi, worm!'" I told this to my sister later, and she said, "He probably would!"

This reminds me of an incident that took place inside my car in a darkened parking lot. I was supposed to meet someone in this restaurant parking lot and get a ride the rest of the way to wherever we were going that day. I don't even remember what that was about. I didn't know if they planned on going somewhere for breakfast, so I stopped and got something. Before I found out I was diabetic, I used to go to the 7-11 near home and get sometimes 1, but usually 2 of those big bar doughnuts with the chocolate frosting and the vanilla pudding inside. Also a big cup of coffee, without sugar. There was enough of that in the doughnuts, even if I hadn't been diabetic.

So here I was in a restaurant parking lot, eating something I hadn't even bought there. I did have dim lighting from the streetlights on the busy street where this place was located, but not enough to really see what I was doing. Therefore, when I spotted what looked like a small string of chocolate icing on my finger, I thought nothing of instantly licking it.

Something was wrong, though. It didn't taste like chocolate; in fact, it didn't taste like much of anything. Just a little rubbery, maybe, but flavorless. Too late, I watched as a small worm curled up and died on my finger. Gross! I licked a worm! I thought it a bit inconsiderate and rude that it would instantly die from my spit. It would have made a great mouthwash commercial, though. Did it die because I didn't use mouthwash, or because their mouthwash that I did use had great antiseptic properties? It could be worked either way.

Speaking of tasting crawly things... recently I was in a popular deli in my area. When I'm in there by myself, I always try to sit at the small table across from the drink refill machine. That way, I can wedge my purse into the spot on the floor between my chair and the wall, and refill my drink without worrying that my purse or the rest of my food will get ripped off when I turn my back. The only trouble is that you do have to put up with intermittent crowds as people come to fill and refill their sodas. That's one reason I go at odd times when most lunch hours from companies are over, or not started yet. Beat the crowds and beat the inconvenience.

A family came in with a kid who was about 7 or 8, and stopped at the drink machine to fill up before either sitting down or leaving to take their food home. I saw the kid put on some phony cardboard glasses with a giant cutout of a spider around the eyeholes. Cardboard legs were sticking out all over. It was probably a Halloween party favor. It didn't seem that there were any lenses in them, though they might have been the kind that had holograms in them, like the Christmas ones they make that show stars or the word, "Joy" when you look at a light. These did seem like empty holes, though. I saw him put them on while he was still facing the drink machine, get them in place, and then turn to face me, hoping for a reaction. He turned around to me, just as I was about to start into the first half of my sandwich. I pretended to flinch in surprise, even though I knew it was coming.

"Do you like spiders?" he asked me.

I decided to jerk his chain. "As long as there's enough ketchup on them," I answered.

"Huh?" He screwed up his face.

"They might be good, as long as you put enough ketchup on them," I rephrased slightly.

A pause, and another, "Huh?" as he turned to his dad. "What'd she say?"

"She said she likes them as long as there's enough ketchup on them."

And then, another screwed up face from the kid, followed by, "Huh?"

Strange, he seemed to be about the perfect age to appreciate that kind of response. My sister's kid would have giggled his head off at that, especially if it had been a few years ago, when he was about the same age as this kid was now. Maybe just because he knows me, and would know what to expect. I think I blew this little guy's mind.

It reminds me of when I told a visiting priest who sometimes fills in for our priest, that I didn't like kids unless they had plenty of mustard on them. He told me he preferred mayonnaise. That *would* be better, huh?

54. Purple Cow Products

I never saw a purple cheese
But still, I know it makes me sneeze!

I never saw no purple butter
But still, I know it makes me sputter!

I never saw no purple milk
But it is *all* of the same ilk!

2005

About the Author

Female, age 47, has lived in California since 1966. Originally from Prairie Village, KS, which most people in the civilized world have never heard of. Has been back to the old neighborhood twice, looking for bumps on the sidewalk, a manhole cover, and assorted playground equipment. Found most of them.

Spends her time writing, house sitting for silly but mostly friendly animals, working on craft projects and checking out ebay for items containing pictures of fruit and vegetables.

All of the enclosed Kiddie Perceptions are true. Don't try this at home unless you're a kid, or don't know any better.